FOUR MONTHS IN LIBBY,

AND THE

CAMPAIGN AGAINST ATLANTA

Capt. J. N. Johnston

Co. H, Sixth Kentucky
Volunteer Infantry

HERITAGE BOOKS
2013

HERITAGE BOOKS
AN IMPRINT OF HERITAGE BOOKS, INC.

Books, CDs, and more—Worldwide

For our listing of thousands of titles see our website
at
www.HeritageBooks.com

A Facsimile Reprint
Published 2013 by
HERITAGE BOOKS, INC.
Publishing Division
5810 Ruatan Street
Berwyn Heights, Md. 20740

Copyright © 1995 Heritage Books, Inc.

Entered, according to Act of Congress, in the year 1864,
by I. N. Johnston
In the Clerk's Office of the District Court
for the Southern District of Ohio

Cincinnati:
Printed at the Methodist Book Concern, for the Author;
R. P. Thompson, Printer, 1864

— Publisher's Notice —

In reprints such as this, it is often not possible to remove blemishes from the original. We feel the contents of this book warrant its reissue despite these blemishes and hope you will agree and read it with pleasure.

International Standard Book Numbers
Paperbound: 978-0-7884-0155-8
Clothbound: 978-0-7884-6874-2

PREFACE.

I MIGHT plead, with truth, "the solicitations of friends" as my apology for appearing in print; but as mine is an unpracticed pen, the public, perhaps, may demand a better reason. Without any crime I have been an inmate of the foulest of Southern prisons, and a companion of the brave men whose condition and treatment has called forth the sympathy of the nation, and which will yet call forth the condemnation of the civilized world. I was one of the party that planned and executed one of the most remarkable escapes known to history—the record of which will be enduring as that of the war itself. The labors and perils of which I was a partaker will, I am well assured, give an interest to these pages which the charm of style can never impart to a tale wanting in stirring incident. I write, then, simply because I have a story to tell, which many will take pleasure in hearing, and which, I doubt not, in after years will employ a more skillful pen than mine.

Those with whom I have sat around the camp-fire, shared the weariness of the march, and the dangers of the battle, will like my story none the less for being plainly told; and my companions in Libby, and the partners of my flight, will think of other matters than brilliant sentences and round periods, as they read these pages. I claim no leadership in the enterprise of which I write—the time has not yet come to give honor to whom honor is due; the reason of my silence in this respect will appear in the course of my narrative.

When I began these pages I had no intention of carrying the reader beyond my escape from Libby. I have, however, been induced to add an account of Sherman's great campaign against Atlanta; and while this will, perhaps, have less interest for the general reader, it will possess more for those who were with me in that memorable march. My friends, I am sure, will be indulgent; may I express the hope that all others will have their sympathies too much aroused for our brave boys, still in prison, to be critical?   I. N. JOHNSTON.

CONTENTS.

CHAPTER I.

ENTERING THE SERVICE.

Character of the age—My own experiences—Object of my book—Entering the service—Elected Captain—The 6th Kentucky—Its deeds...................PAGE 9

CHAPTER II.

SHILOH AND STONE RIVER.

My first battle, and how I felt—Wounded and left on the field—Disasters of first day and final triumph................... 21

CHAPTER III.

CHICKAMAUGA.

The battle—Am taken prisoner—Trip to Richmond—Incidents on the way—Star-Spangled Banner sung in Dixie—Kind treatment—Arrival at Richmond........................... 33

CHAPTER IV.

FAILURES.

Richmond—The prison—Treatment of Prisoners—Plans of escape—Sad Failures—Prospect of success....................... 46

CHAPTER V.

THE TUNNEL.

A new plan adopted—Nature of the task—In the tunnel—Maj. M'Donald's adventure—My own disappearance—Given up as escaped—Fislar's story .... PAGE 65

CHAPTER VI.

CELLAR LIFE.

My home and company—Great alarm—Still safe—The work renewed—Success—Last night in Libby—Words on leaving. 81

CHAPTER VII.

THE ESCAPE.

The last night—Farewell to Libby—Sufferings and dangers—The North Star our guide—The faithful negro—A false friend—Almost retaken—The contrast 95

CHAPTER VIII.

UNDER THE FLAG AGAIN.

In the swamp—Meeting our pickets—Warm welcome—Kind treatment—Interview with General Butler—Arrival at Washington 113

CHAPTER IX.

RETURN TO THE FRONT.

Return home—How I spent my furlough—Join my regiment—Changes—Forward movement—Tunnel Hill—Rocky Face—Resaca 127

CONTENTS.

CHAPTER X.

ON TO ATLANTA.

Confidence in our leader—Tunnel Hill and Rocky Face Mountain—Pursuit of the enemy—Johnston's strategy—In command of my regiment—Battle near Dallas—Night on the battle-field—Reflections...................................PAGE 142

CHAPTER XI.

MARCHING AND FIGHTING.

Reminder to the reader—Sherman, Howard, and Thomas in council—The attack and repulse—The Sixth Kentucky in front again—In the trenches—Guarding train—Forward march. 155

CHAPTER XII.

SHERMAN STILL FLANKING.

Pine Mountain and death of Gen. Polk—Georgia scenery—Before Kenesaw—The unreturning brave—Marietta ours—Across the Chattahoochee.. 167

CHAPTER XIII.

BEFORE ATLANTA.

Intrenching all night—Gallant exploit of the First and Third Brigades—Atlanta in view—In the trenches before the city—The Sixth Kentucky ordered to Tennessee—Turning over my command—A parting word............................ 180

FOUR MONTHS IN LIBBY.

CHAPTER I.

ENTERING THE SERVICE.

Character of the age—My own experiences—Object of my book—Entering the service—Elected captain—The 6th Kentucky—Its deeds.

I AM a soldier, a plain, blunt man; hence, what I have to say will have the directness of a soldier's tale. The age in which we live is a heroic one; boys who four years ago were at school or guiding the plow are now heroes; we have battle-fields enough for all time, and names on the page of history eclipsing those of the great captains of the past—names that the world will not willingly let die. Reason as we may, there is a charm about the story of a great war that few are able to resist; grave scholars go into ecstasies over the tale of Troy; and the youth, whose reading is confined to the old family Bible, devours with avidity those portions which tell of the exploits of Samson or the triumphs of David; and it is the fearful conflicts which they describe that give such interest to the Paradise Lost and Bunyan's Holy War. What boy's blood has not been stirred by the story of Bunker Hill, the exploits of a Marion, and the fall of Yorktown? What youth has not wept as he read the story of Warren's death, or the sadder story of the execution of Hale, the proud young martyr of liberty? and in generations to come the youth of this land, with burning cheek and tearful eye, will read how Ellsworth fell, just as he had torn down the emblem of treason; and how the gallant young Dahlgren died, almost in sight of the sad captives whom he desired to deliver. Who has not been thrilled with horror at the cruelties inflicted by the minions of the British King upon the colonists taken in arms for a cause the most noble, and consigned to the living grave of the prison-ship? and yet these cruelties have been repeated, with even increased malignity, at Belle Isle and Libby Prison.

I have experienced nearly all the fortunes of a soldier, and can therefore speak from my own personal observation. I have felt that ardent love of country which has taken so many from the peaceful pursuits of life to the tented field. I know something of the stern joy of battle, the rapture of victory; I am familiar with the long, weary march, want of food, and thirst, which amounts to agony; nay, I have been stretched almost lifeless on the battlefield, know something of the long, weary hours of slow recovery from painful wounds, and, harder than all, long months of sad, weary, and almost hopeless captivity, and the joy, too, of escape from what almost seemed a living tomb. And though young, wanting the large experience of some, and the culture of others; yet my plain, unadorned story, I feel well assured, will not be told in vain.

I shall make no apology, then, for any literary defects; the work I propose is not one of art or imagination, but a record of facts; and in whatever other respects it may fail, it will, at least, have the merit of truth. Moreover, I write mainly for my companions in arms, my comrades by whose sides I have fought, and with whom I have suffered; and if, in fighting over again our battles, rehearsing our common dangers, privations, toils, and triumphs, I can minister to their pleasure, my task will not be a useless one, and my little book will long be a link to bind together hearts that danger has only endeared.

Nor am I without hope that I shall be able to awaken an interest for the soldier in the minds of those who never have passed through scenes such as I describe. He who unselfishly bares his breast to the storm of battle, who

ENTERING THE SERVICE.

stands between peaceful homes and danger, who suffers that others may be safe, certainly deserves well of his country; and never have any soldiers established a better claim on the gratitude of their country than the soldiers of the Union. As a nation, we have honored the men who achieved our independence: we ought never to forget those who struck for home and native land, when all that the heart holds dear was imperiled, and the very life of the nation threatened by armed traitors.

If a man's acts are regarded as the exponents of his patriotism, mine, I feel assured, will not be questioned, and yet at the same time I feel at perfect liberty to honor kindness, truth, and magnanimity in a foe; and wherever these are found, even in an enemy, I shall not be slow to acknowledge it. Having now, as I trust, established a good understanding between myself and readers, I shall proceed to cultivate still further their acquaintance by a free and unreserved statement of whatever may seem to be of interest prior to my life in Libby.

Like thousands of my fellow-soldiers, I am a farmer's son. The only college with which I have had any acquaintance is the old-fashioned log school-house; and a few years ago I as little dreamed of being an author as I did of being a soldier; my only literary achievements heretofore have been sundry epistles to the fairer portion of creation, and in that department I am not able to declare positively that the pen is mightier than the sword, as I rather incline to the opinion that few things have more influence with that portion of humanity than soldierly bearing and a suit of Federal blue. And had I rested my claims to their favor upon authorship, I fear it would have proved but a broken reed. My military career, however, I have not found to be an impediment, and even an unsightly wound was not a deformity in the eyes of her who was dearest to me.

You will be disappointed, kind reader, if you expect from me a history of the causes of the war. I am not sufficiently skilled in the political history of the country for such an undertaking, and, indeed, there is no necessity for it, as it has already been done by far abler hands than mine. Still, in a contest like the present, every man should have reasons for his course, especially when that course involves personal danger and sacrifices the greatest a man can make—sacrifices which, if need require, must not stop short of life itself.

My own reasons are those of thousands of others, but they are not those of the mere politician; they are the reasons of the man and the patriot who loves his country with an unselfish love, and loves that country most, not in the days of peace and prosperity, but when the clouds are darkest and perils and trials beset her round. A milder, freer Government than ours the world never saw; we knew not that we had a Government, by any burdens that it imposed upon us; it was only by the constant flow of blessings we enjoyed that we were conscious of its existence. Our history, though short, was glorious; our future full of the brightest promise, and the hopes of the toiling and oppressed millions of Europe were bound up in our success.

Though not an adept in the theory of government, I could not be blind to its practical workings; though no politician, I could not be insensible of the manifold blessings which it secured. I remembered the wisdom of those men who gave shape to our institutions; I remembered the price at which independence was purchased; I remembered that it was not without blood that those blessings were gained; and now that all that the wisdom of a Franklin, Hancock, and Adams had devised—all that for which a Washington had fought, for which Warren had bled, was in jeopardy, I felt that in such a cause, and for such a country, it would be sweet even to die.

No love of war and bloodshed led me to the field; the charter of our independence was sealed with blood, the very blessings of civil and religious liberty which we enjoy I felt to be purchased by noble lives freely given; and to preserve them for generations yet to come I felt to be worth as great a sacrifice. God grant that the effort may not be in vain! God grant that the fierce struggle which has filled our land with weeping may be followed by all the blessings of a lasting peace!

Under the influence of the sentiments just expressed, no sooner was the flag of my country insulted, and an attempt made by bold, bad men to pull down the fairest fabric ever devised by human wisdom and cemented by patriot blood, than I determined to do my utmost to uphold the starry banner; and seeking no position save that of one of my country's defenders, I volunteered for three years. Nearly one hundred young men, mostly from my own locality—Henry county, Ky.—enrolled themselves at the same time, and became soldiers of the Union. We all had much around us to render life pleasant, and home dear; but the call of our country in her hour of need sounded in our ears, and we could not permit her to call in vain. After the organization of our regiment—the Sixth Kentucky Volunteer Infantry—the young men from my part of the county selected me as their captain, and I have had the honor of commanding Company H, of the Sixth Kentucky Volunteer Infantry, till the present time. I have been with that company in several of the bloodiest battles of the war, and in a number of severe skirmishes; and having seen its members time and again under the enemy's fire, I take pleasure in saying that a better and braver band of men never shouldered muskets or faced a foe upon the battle-plain. Indeed, the Sixth Kentucky has a record of which it may well be proud; its steady endurance in resisting an attack, and its fiery valor when hurling its ranks on the foe, has covered it with well-deserved renown. Shiloh, Stone River, and Mission Ridge have witnessed its prowess; its ranks have been thinned in many a fierce and bloody assault, and of those who yet follow its flag to victory, and of those who fill a soldier's grave, it shall be said, they were heroes, every one.

And yet it checks our exultation, brings tears to the eyes and sadness to the heart to think of the sad ravages that war has made in the ranks of those noble men. Where are they now? Some have met death on the field, and fill unmarked graves far, far from home; others escaped death on the field to perish by slow, wasting disease in camp and hospital. Some, with mutilated limbs and features disfigured with ghastly wounds, have sought the rest, quiet, and sympathy of home; while others in rebel prisons drag out a wretched existence, feeling all the pain and heart-sickness of hope deferred. On earth many of them will meet no more; yet, when the survivors meet in the years which are to come, when the sounds of strife have ceased, they will speak in low tones of the cherished dead, and drop a tear to their memory, and remember with pride that they themselves were on many a well-fought field with the Sixth Kentucky.

CHAPTER II.

SHILOH AND STONE RIVER.

My first battle, and how I felt—Wounded and left on the field—Disasters of first day and final triumph—Return home—In the field again—Battle of Stone River—Wounded again—Appearance of the country.

My first battle! What a strange sensation it was when I knew that I must soon engage in the deadly strife! The thoughts came thick and fast—thoughts of home, friends, and loved ones crowded upon me with a vividness and distinctness I had never known before. My past life came up in review, and the anxiety to know the result of the next few hours was painful. Should I fall on my first field, or should I escape? Should I share the joy of victory, or experience the sadness of defeat? be a prisoner in the hands of the foe, or, wounded, lie helpless among the slain and dying? make myself a name, or fill a nameless grave, were questions that would force themselves upon my attention. Fearful I was not, but excited, as every one doubtless is when about to enter for the first time the field of carnage and blood.

I can imagine a young soldier gradually becoming accustomed to warfare by engaging at first in slight skirmishes at long range, then in closer encounters, till he is, in a measure, prepared for a general engagement; but my first battle was none of those, but one of the great conflicts of the war, in which thousands went in tyros in the art of war, and came out heroes, ever after confident and bold—it was the bloody field of Shiloh.

It is difficult, perhaps impossible, to describe a battle; one pair of eyes can see but little of a conflict ranging over miles of territory; but there is something common to all battles which every brave man sees and hears, such as the shrieking of the shells, the blaze which accompanies the explosion, the whistling of minie balls, the clash and clang of steel, the roar of the artillery, the rattle of musketry, comrades falling, riderless steeds dashing hither and thither, the shout of officers, the hurrah of the charging line, the ghastly forms of the dead, the piteous cries of the wounded, the clouds of smoke pierced by the quick flashes of flame—with all these every true soldier is familiar.

Our regiment was not in the battle the first day, but came up the following night, and found Gen. Grant, who had been hard pressed the preceding day, in grim silence awaiting the coming light to renew the contest. Early in the morning we were engaged, and the battle raged with great fury till the middle of the afternoon, when the enemy, after a stubborn resistance, were routed, and a shout of triumph went up from the victors who had changed threatened disaster into glorious success.

In that shout of joy I took no part—nay, I heard it as if in a dream; for about twelve or one o'clock a minie ball, striking me on the left cheek, passing through and coming out an inch behind and below the ear, laid me for a time unconscious on the field amid the dead and the dying. Reviving after awhile I slowly made my way to the rear amid a shower of leaden and iron hail. The loss in my company was one killed and fifteen or sixteen wounded, several of them mortally. This battle, as most readers are aware, began on Sunday, the 6th of April. Early in the morning the Confederate forces, in greatly-superior numbers, under Generals A. S. Johnston and Beauregard, attacked Gen. Grant with great fury, the divisions of Sherman, M'Clernand, and Prentiss were driven back, and their respective camps fell into the hands of the enemy. They were stubbornly resisted, however, by Gen. Wallace's division, already weakened by having sent a brigade to assist in another portion of the field.

These brave fellows nobly repulsed four different attacks made upon them, each time inflicting a heavy loss on the foe; but when night fell much ground had been lost, and many a heart was anxious concerning the morrow. During the night, however, Buell came up, a heavy burden was removed from many minds; for those who had hitherto contemplated nothing more than a stubborn resistance now felt confident of victory. Nor were they disappointed; the arrival of new troops infused fresh vigor into those wearied with the desperate struggle of the preceding day, and ere the sun had set the enemy had scattered before their resistless advance, the lost ground was all recovered, the lost camps retaken, and the roads southward thronged with a fleeing foe. Johnston, the rebel commander-in-chief, was killed upon the field on the first day; and though Beauregard claimed a complete victory on the 6th, and the rebel capital was wild with joy on the reception of his bulletin, he was compelled the next day to retire in disorder and seek safety within his fortifications at Corinth.

As soon as I was sufficiently recovered to be removed, I was sent home to Kentucky for treatment. I reached there faint and weary, was seized with typhoid fever, which, together with wounds, came very near terminating my life. My first battle, however, was not destined to be my last, and, by skillful treatment, careful nursing, and the interposition of a kind Providence, I was finally restored.

As soon as I was able I rejoined my company; was with it during Buell's march through Tennessee and Kentucky to Louisville; bore its privations well; was in hearing of the battle of Perryville, but our regiment was not engaged. From Perryville we marched through Danville, skirmishing with Bragg's rear-guard; thence to Crab Orchard and Stanford; harassed him as far as London, Laurel county — turned back, marched to Glasgow, thence to Nashville, where we arrived about the 1st of December, 1862.

My first battle, as I have already stated, was under Grant and Buell, against Johnston and Beauregard; my second was against Bragg at Stone River, under Rosecrans. Here, again, it was my fate or fortune to be wounded—this time in three places; but none of my wounds were severe enough to make me leave the field. Both my arms were bruised by fragments of bombshells, another piece struck my pistol which hung by my side, tearing the stock to atoms and bending the iron nearly double. I was knocked down by the violence of the blow, and received a pretty severe wound in my side, and I have no doubt but the pistol saved my life. I had my blanket over my shoulders during the engagement, and at its close I found that four or five balls had passed through it, several bullets also had pierced my coat, and in looking at them I seemed to realize how near to death I had been, and felt devoutly thankful that I had escaped the dangers of another fierce struggle. Soldiers look with pride at the flag, pierced by the bullets of the foe, which they have proudly borne through the din and smoke of battle, and in that feeling I have often partaken; but I shall ever feel grateful to a kind Providence whenever I look at my bullet-pierced blanket and coat; and if I fall before the war closes, I wish no more fitting and honorable shroud than these will afford; if I survive, they shall be preserved as relics of that eventful day, as silent monitors to teach me thankfulness to Him whose hand protected me in the hour of danger.

The battle of Stone River began on the 31st of December, 1862, and continued till the evening of the 2d of January. On the first day our left wing was driven back, and we lost about thirty pieces of artillery; but the attack of the enemy on our center was repelled with fearful slaughter, being subjected to a terrible cross-fire of double-shotted canister from two batteries, and the day closed with the contest undecided. The next day the battle was renewed, our line being restored to the position it had occupied on the morning of the previous day, but without any very decisive result, the spirit of our forces remaining unbroken. On the third day attempts were made by the enemy along our whole line, but it was not till about the middle of the afternoon, however, that the crisis of the battle came; both sides were using their artillery with terrible effect; at last the line of the enemy began to give way; Gen. Davis was ordered to charge across the stream from which the battle takes its name; the Colonel of the 78th Pennsylvania, with his hat on the point of his sword, led the way with a hurrah, a charge perfectly irresistible was made, the enemy's line was broken, the divisions of Beatty and Negley came up rapidly, our whole line advanced and the day was won.

My wounds gave me some inconvenience for a few days; but as I had been much more severely wounded before, I did not regard them much, having learned to look upon them as the necessary accompaniments of a soldier's life; indeed, they were soon forgotten, and I was soon again ready for the duties of my position. It is truly wonderful with what facility man adapts himself to circumstances; one would think that such constant exposure to danger and to death would beget great seriousness in every mind, and yet the reverse seems to be the case; after having been under fire a few times, the soldier goes into battle with an alacrity and cheerfulness that is astonishing; he becomes inured to the sight of wounds and death, and though his comrades fall on either side, and he has a sigh for them, he thinks not that he, like them, may fall. On the march, however, sad thoughts often come.

The country between Murfreesboro and Nashville is a beautiful one, but the rude hand of war has despoiled it of much of its loveliness. Fire is a necessity to the soldier, and no fuel is so ready to his hand as fence-rails, and wherever the army marches the fences rapidly disappear; thousands upon thousands of fertile acres are thus left without any protection, beautiful shrubbery and choice fruit trees are ruined, every green thing is taken from the gardens, fowls and domestic animals are killed, and the country which lately bloomed like a garden becomes as desolate as a barren desert. Little mounds by the roadside tell that those dear to some hearts are buried there; dead horses, broken wagons tell of the waste of war; traces of fire and solitary chimney-stacks bring up images of homes once pleasant, and cause the wish and prayer for the return of peace. Soldiers are sometimes thought to exaggerate the scenes through which they pass; but let any one who has seen Tennessee in the days of its prosperity travel from Nashville to Chattanooga now, and he will confess that no pen can de scribe, much less exaggerate, the scenes everywhere presented to the eye. But a truce to moralizing. After the retreat of the foe the monotony of camp life began to be oppressive; a desire for active operations, no matter by what dangers attended, became general, and in this feeling I confess I shared. The desired change came at length, and with it a disaster greater far than sickness or wounds—the sufferings of a long and painful captivity, such captivity as the dwellers in that synonym for all that is foul and loathsome—Libby Prison—alone have known.

CHAPTER III.

CHICKAMAUGA.

The battle—Am taken prisoner—Trip to Richmond—Incidents on the way—Star-Spangled Banner sung in Dixie—Kind treatment—Arrival at Richmond.

THE battle of Chickamauga, one of the most stoutly contested of the war, may be said to have commenced on Friday, the 18th of September, 1863; but the heaviest fighting took place on Saturday and Sunday. We were outnumbered, as is well known; but, by the persistent courage of Gen. Thomas and his brave associates, the enemy were foiled in their purpose—which was to retake Chattanooga—and the army saved from the disaster which at one time during the fight seemed inevitable. Bragg, it is true, claimed a glorious victory; but if battles are to be judged by their results, his victory was a fruitless one, the prize which was at stake remaining in our hands. True, we lost many brave men, and much of the material of war; but Chattanooga, the key of Georgia, was not wrested from our grasp; the valor of the troops, too, was never more nobly illustrated; for the stout men under Thomas stood unshaken on Mission Ridge as the wave-washed rock, against which the hitherto invincible legions of Longstreet, like fierce billows, madly dashed themselves, to fall back, like those broken billows, in foam and spray.

Men fell upon that field whose names never will perish, and others, who still live, there gained immortal renown. There fell Lytle, the poet-hero; sweet was his lyre, and strong was his sword. There the modest yet brave Thomas displayed the qualities of a great general, firm and undismayed amid carnage and threatened disaster; and there Garfield, the gallant and the good, won richly-deserved honor.

But to my own story. I had been unwell for several days, but the excitement of the conflict aroused and sustained me. Late on the evening of Saturday our brigade was ordered to retreat, and, unable to keep up with the main body, I was overtaken and captured. I was taken in charge by two lieutenants, and regret that I did not learn their names or command, as they treated me with marked kindness, as brave men ever treat a conquered foe. They saw, moreover, by my appearance, that I was quite ill, and this doubtless excited their sympathy. Soon another lieutenant came up; he was a Georgian, and drunk; he took away my sword-belt and haversack. Being cautioned by the others to take care of my watch, I slipped it down my back unobserved by my Georgia friend, and saved it for the time being. My captors conducted me about a mile and a half to the rear, and kept me there all night. We had to pass over the ground that had been fought over during the day; it was thickly strewed with the dead and wounded of both armies; their dead seemed to be in the proportion of three to our one. I saw Gen. Bragg for the first time at a distance. The night was intensely cold for the season, and I suffered severely, having lost my blanket; moreover, I was exhausted from hunger, having eaten nothing for two days. I was fortunate enough, however, to meet with a prisoner of the 9th Indiana, who generously gave me a cup of coffee and a cracker, after which I felt greatly refreshed. This noble fellow also shared his scanty covering with me, and I trust he may ever find a friend as kind as he proved to me. By morning the number of prisoners was quite large, most of them nearly starved; the men guarding us were very kind, and said they would gladly give us food, but they were as destitute and as hungry as ourselves. To prove their sincerity they marched us to a sweet-potato patch, and all hands, prisoners and guards, in army phrase, "pitched in." We then made fires and roasted the potatoes, and often since have made a worse meal. We were then marched across the Chickamauga River to a white house, where we found another lot of prisoners collected; our names were taken, and every man was relieved of his haversack; they were taken by a Texas captain, who distributed them to his own men. This was Sunday, the 20th. About ten o'clock in the morning the battle commenced again, and we prisoners were ordered into rank and marched in the direction of Ringgold. After an hour's march we were halted till about two in the afternoon, during which time there was another squad of prisoners marched to the rear and added to our number. During all this time the battle was raging furiously, and as the sound of the fierce conflict came to our ears there was the greatest anxiety on the part of our guard as well as ourselves. I had heard that Rosecrans had been heavily reënforced, and believing it to be true, was sanguine of success.

At two o'clock the captured officers, now numbering about one hundred and fifty, were ordered to fall in according to rank, non-commissioned officers and privates to follow. In this order we marched, stopping a few minutes to rest at the end of every hour, stimulated by the promise that we should draw rations as soon as we reached Ringgold. On our way we met one of Longstreet's brigades hurrying to the front; they were fine, soldierly-looking men, the very flower of the Confederate army, better drilled and equipped than any Southern troops I had seen, either at Shiloh or Stone River; they were confident, too, from their successes in Virginia; but they found their equals, at least, at Mission Ridge in the gallant men of the West. We reached Ringgold about nine o'clock at night, but failed to draw the promised rations, and were told if we would march four miles further we should come to the

CHICKAMAUGA. 39

camp of a brigade of Longstreet's men, who were guarding a railroad station, and be sure to find the much-desired rations there. Many of us had been nearly worn out marching previous to the battle, and had passed through one day's fight; nevertheless, so hungry were we, that we were glad to drag our weary limbs four miles further, and in that distance wade the Chickamauga three times, in the hope of finding food, fire, and rest.

When within a short distance of the camp we were ordered to take rails from a fence to make fires to dry our clothes and make ourselves comfortable for the night. We were eager to avail ourselves of the liberty thus granted, and soon a column of men, about two thousand in number, each with from three to five rails on his shoulder, were marching on. About two o'clock in the morning, wet, dispirited, and weary, we reached camp, wincing somewhat under the burden of our rails, which grew heavier every step. Again we were doomed to disappointment; we found nothing there to relieve our hunger; so we kindled our fires, stretched ourselves near them, and strove to forget the pangs of hunger and the bitterness of captivity in sleep.

On the morning of the 21st we were marched to Tunnel Hill, a distance of five miles. We remained there till two P. M., in which interval the long-desired rations of corn meal and bacon were issued. We asked for time to bake our bread and divide the meat, and were assured that we should have the opportunity we desired. Men were detailed to bake the bread and cut up the bacon, and in imagination we saw the long-expected and welcome meal prepared; but scarcely were our fires lighted and the meat divided, before we were again ordered into ranks, and obliged to leave nearly all our uncooked rations lying on the ground. To famishing men this was a severe trial; but orders were imperative, and with sad hearts we marched to the depot, where we found a train of cars awaiting our arrival. We got on board and reached Kingston, where we remained till morning. Here we met a brigade of Longstreet's men, who treated us with great kindness, many of them dividing their rations with us.

The same day we moved forward to Atlanta, which place we reached at five, P. M. We found an immense crowd awaiting the arrival of the Yankees, and were stared at and criticised in a manner far from agreeable. Pity for our condition dwelt in the hearts of some, but they were forced to restrain any expression of sympathy; while those who came to jeer, and laugh, and to show their mean exultation, gratified their feelings to the fullest extent. We were marched to a dirty hill-side a short distance from the city, and surrounded by a strong guard. Our camp inclosed a spring in its limits, but had very little wood for fuel; the absence of this we felt keenly, as the nights were cold, and we without tents or blankets, and many of us having lost our overcoats, and thus left without any thing to protect us in our dismal quarters beneath the open sky. Some time after nightfall we received a small ration of bread and beef, the first which we had been permitted to cook and eat for four days, during which time we had subsisted on raw corn and elderberries, which we gathered at the different points at which we had stopped on our way from the battle-field. The officers in charge of us said that the reason we were not supplied with food before, was, that they were nearly destitute themselves, which was doubtless true, as our guards fared just as we did.

We remained at our dirty and disagreeable camp till the afternoon of the next day, when we were removed to the barracks, where we were searched. Many citizens, both male and female, gratified their curiosity by calling to see us, doubtless expecting, from the reports they had heard, to see a race of beings far different from themselves. The next morning we were ordered to take the cars for Richmond. Previous to starting for the depot we had selected several stirring National songs, which we sung as we passed through the city. This demonstration attracted great attention; windows were thrown up, doorways thronged, and soon even the streets crowded with citizens, who came rushing from every direction to hear those unusual strains. Many scowled upon us as we went singing by, while some smiled approvingly, as if delighted to hear once more the songs of the Union; and for my own part the Star-Spangled Banner fell more sweetly upon my ear, though far down South, a prisoner and among the enemies of that flag, than ever before. Strange to say, we were not interrupted; and as the boys joined in the swelling chorus, with heads erect and hearts high beating, they seemed more like victors returning from glorious fields, than captives on their way to a gloomy prison, to be exchanged by many of them for an untimely grave—nay, not untimely; for those who perished there were no less heroes and martyrs than those who laid down their lives on the field of honor—not one of them has died in vain.

Leaving Atlanta, we reached Augusta about twelve o'clock at night, and were marched to a church-yard, in which we camped till next morning. We were well treated by the citizens; many of them visited us, and showed us such kindness during our stay, that we could not but conclude that many of them, at heart, were lovers of the Union still. Nor was this the only occasion, while passing through the South, that we discovered strong symptoms of a Union sentiment among the people; many have secretly cherished the sacred flame, and will yet welcome the army of the Union as their deliverers. Leaving Augusta, we crossed the Savannah River into South Carolina, passed through Raleigh,

Weldon, and Petersburg, and on the 29th of September, about seven o'clock in the evening, we reached the depot at Richmond, and were marched to our Libby home.

CHAPTER IV.

FAILURES.

Richmond—The prison—Treatment of prisoners—Employment—Plans of escape—Sad failures—Prospect of success.

During our trip from Chickamauga to Richmond the weather was clear and beautiful, but the nights were cold, and many of us, having lost our blankets, suffered much; for, in addition to the want of our usual covering, we were hungry nearly all the time. Many of the cities and towns through which we passed presented a pleasing appearance; but the country, for the most part, had a desolate look; few men were to be seen, save such as were too old for service, and the farming operations bore marks of neither care nor skill.

The officer who had the prisoners in charge

was kind and gentlemanly, and rendered our situation as agreeable as was possible under the circumstances; that we suffered for food was no fault of his, and when we were turned over to the authorities at Richmond we parted from him with a feeling akin to regret.

All the private soldiers were sent to Belle Isle, a place which has become infamous on account of the cruel treatment to which they were subjected; but the officers had quarters assigned them in Libby Prison. Before being shown to our apartments we were requested to give up our money and valuables, under the assurance that they should be returned when we were exchanged; at the same time we were given to understand that we should be searched, and whatever was then found in our possession would be confiscated. Nearly all gave up what they had; some secreted a portion, which was found to be clear gain, as those of us who escaped had not time to call for our money and watches before leaving for the Federal lines.

This now world-famous building presents none of the outward characteristics of a prison, having been used in peaceful days as a warehouse; but none of the castles and dungeons of Europe, century old though they be, have a stranger or sadder history than this. There many a heart has been wrung, many a spirit broken, many a noble soul has there breathed out its last sigh, and hundreds who yet survive will shrink in their dreams, or shudder in their waking moments, when faithful memory brings back the scenes enacted within its fearful walls. The building is of brick, with a front of near one hundred and forty feet, and one hundred feet deep. It is divided into nine rooms; the ceilings are low, and ventilation imperfect; the windows are barred, through which the windings of James River and the tents of Belle Isle may be seen. Its immediate surroundings are far from being agreeable; the sentinels pacing the streets constantly are unpleasant reminders that your stay is not a matter of choice; and were it so, few would choose it long as a boarding-house.

In this building were crowded about one thousand officers of nearly every grade, not one of whom was permitted to go out till exchanged or released by death. To men accustomed to an active life this mode of existence soon became exceedingly irksome, and innumerable methods were soon devised to make the hours pass less wearily. A penknife was made to do the duty of a complete set of tools, and it was marvelous to see the wonders achieved by that single instrument. Bone-work of strange device, and carving most elaborate, chess-men, spoons, pipes, all manner of articles, useful and ornamental, were fashioned by its aid alone. If a man's early education had been neglected, ample opportunities were now afforded to become a proficient scholar. The higher branches of learning had their professor; the languages, ancient and modern, were taught; mathematics received much attention; morals and religion were cared for in Bible classes, while the ornamental branches, such as dancing, vocal music, and sword exercise, had had their teachers and pupils. Indeed, few colleges in the land could boast of a faculty so large in number or varied in accomplishments, and none, certainly, could compare in the number of pupils.

But truth must be told; the minds of many of those grown-up, and, in some instances, gray-headed pupils, were not always with their books; their minds, when children, wandered from the page before them to the green fields, to streams abounding in fish, or pleasant for bathing; or to orchards, with fruit most inviting; but now the mind wandered in one direction—home. Others were deeply engaged in the mysteries of "poker" and "seven-up," and betting ran high; but they were bets involving neither loss or gain, and the winner of countless sums would often borrow a teaspoon full of salt or a pinch of pepper. Games of chess were played, which, judging from the wary and deliberate manner of the players, and the interest displayed by lookers-on, were as intricate and important as a military campaign; nor were the sports of children—jack-straws and mumble-peg—wanting; every device, serious and silly, was employed to hasten the slow hours along. But amid all these various occupations, there was one that took the precedence and absorbed all others—that was planning an escape. The exploits of Jack Sheppard, Baron Trenck, and the hero of Monte Cristo were seriously considered, and plans superior to theirs concocted, some of them characterized by skill and cunning, others by the energy of despair.

One of these was as follows: After the arrival of the Chickamauga prisoners, a plot was made which embraced the escape of all confined in Libby, and the release of all the prisoners in and about Richmond. The leader in this enterprise was a man of cool purpose and great daring; and success, I doubt not, would have attended the effort had it not been that we had traitors in our midst who put the rebel authorities on the alert only a few days before the attempt was to have been made.

Prisoners, it is true, have no right to expect abundant and delicious fare; but when the rations served out to rebel prisoners in our hands are compared with the stinted and disgusting allowance of Union prisoners in rebel hands, a truly-generous and chivalrous people would blush at the contrast. It is not saying too much to assert that many of the rebel prisoners, from the poorer portions of Georgia, South Carolina, and Mississippi, have, at least, as good fare, and as much of it, as they ever enjoyed at home, and much better than the army rations which they were accustomed to before capture; while it is equally true that the Union prisoners have been compelled to subsist on a diet loathsome in quality, and in a quantity scarcely sufficient to support life. True, it may be urged that the scarcity of provisions in Richmond, and elsewhere, rendered it out of the question to remedy this to any great extent; but all candid men will decide that no army could be kept, in the physical condition of Gen. Lee's, upon a Libby ration; and if such a miracle as that were possible, it would not justify the denial to prisoners of the Union army the provisions that the United States were ever ready to furnish their own men while prisoners in an enemy's hands, much less the appropriation of the stores sent to those sufferers by benevolent associations and sympathizing friends. That vast quantities of food and clothing sent to our prisoners has been thus diverted from its object, is susceptible of the clearest proof. If it be asked, how can a people, professing to be civilized, act thus? the answer is simply, that the war, as far as the South is concerned, is a rebellion.

The Libby ration nominally consisted of about ten ounces of corn bread—of meal just as it came from the mill—beef, and rice; but really less often than this; for it often took two rations of beef to make a single tolerable meal, and frequently we would fail to get any beef for from one to eight days; at such times we would receive sweet or Irish potatoes; and I state the case very mildly when I say the food was at all times insufficient. Of wood for cooking purposes we had a very small allowance; and during the Christmas holidays we had to burn our tables in attempting to make palatable dishes out of very scanty and unpalatable materials. One thing, however, we did not lack; the James River was near at hand, and we had plenty of water; it was brought by means of pipes into each room; and had it possessed any very nutritious properties, we might have fattened. I must do the officers of the prison the justice to say, that as long as we did not violate the rules of the house, they permitted us to enjoy ourselves in any way that suited our taste. Prayer meetings and debating societies were tolerated, laughter and song in certain hours were not prohibited, and bad as our condition was, it might have been even worse.

Our first plan of escape being thwarted, no time was lost in devising another, which, after many delays and interruptions of a very discouraging character, was finally crowned with success. Captain Hamilton, of the 12th Kentucky Cavalry, was the author of the plan, which he confided to Maj. Fitzsimmons, of the 30th Indiana, Capt. Gallagher, of the 2d Ohio, and a third person, whose name it would not be prudent to mention, as he was recaptured. I greatly regret to pass him by with this brief allusion, as he had a very prominent part in the work from the beginning, and deserves far more credit than I have language to express. As this, however, is one of the most wonderful escapes on record, when its complete history is written he will not be forgotten. John Morgan's escape from the Ohio Penitentiary has been thought to have suggested our plan, and to have equaled it in ingenuity and risk. His difficulties, however, ended when he emerged from the tunnel by which he escaped, while ours may be said to have only begun when we reached the free air, and every step till we reached the Union lines was fraught with great danger.

After Capt. Hamilton's plans had been intrusted to and adopted by the gentlemen above named, a solemn pledge was taken to reveal them to none others, and at an early date in December, 1863, the work was begun.

In order to a perfect understanding of it, a more minute description of the building is necessary. It is not far from one hundred and forty feet by one hundred and ten, three stories high, and divided into three departments by heavy brick walls. The divisions were occupied as follows: The two upper east rooms by the Potomac officers, the two middle upper rooms by those captured at Chickamauga, the two west upper rooms by the officers of Col. Streight's and Gen. Milroy's command; the lower room of the east division was used as a hospital, the lower middle room for a cook and dining-room, and the lower west is divided into several apartments which were occupied by the rebel officers in command. There is also a cellar under each of these divisions; the east cellar was used for commissary stores, such as meal, turnips, fodder, and straw—the latter article was of vast benefit in effecting our escape. The rear and darker part of the middle cellar was cut up into cells, to which were consigned those of our number who were guilty of infractions of the rules of prison— dungeons dark and horrible beyond description. The portion of it in front was used as a workshop, and the west cellar was used for cooking the rations of private soldiers who were confined in other buildings, and as quarters for some negro captives who were kept to do the drudgery of the prison.

As the plan was to dig out, it became necessary to find a way into the east cellar, from which to begin our tunnel, which was accomplished as follows. Near the north end of the dining-room was a fireplace, around which three large cooking stoves were arranged. In this fireplace the work began. The bricks were skillfully taken out, and through this aperture a descent to the east cellar was effected. This part of the work was intrusted to Captains Hamilton and Gallagher, who were both house-builders, and in their hands it was a perfect success. The only tools used were pocket-knives; consequently their progress was slow, and fifteen nights elapsed before the place was reached where the tunnel was to begin. The stoves mentioned above aided greatly in the prosecution of the work, screening the operators from observation. Immediately in front of them the prisoners had a dancing party nearly every night, and the light of their tallow candles made the stoves throw a dark shadow over the entrance to the newly-opened way to the cellar, and the mirth of the dancers drowned any slight noise that might be made by the working party. Considerable skill was necessary in order to reach the cellar after the opening was made; and on one occasion one of the party stuck fast, and was released only by great efforts on the part of his associates. Poor fellow! though fortunate enough to escape detection in this instance, and afterward to reach the free air, he was recaptured and taken back to a confinement more intolerable than before.

The cellar being reached, a thorough examination was made in order to decide upon a route which would be most favorable for our escape; and it was determined to make an attempt in the rear of a cook-room which was in the south-east corner of the cellar. The plan was to dig down and pass under the foundation, then change the direction and work parallel with the wall to a large sewer that passes down Canal-street, and from thence make our escape. The attempt was accordingly made; but it was soon discovered that the building rested upon ponderous oak timbers, below which they could not penetrate. Determined to succeed, they began the seemingly-hopeless task of cutting through these; pocket-knives and saws made out of case-knives were the only available tools; and when this, after much hard labor, was effected, they were met by an unforeseen and still more serious difficulty. Water began to flow into the tunnel; a depth below the level of the canal had been reached, and sadly they were compelled to abandon the undertaking. A second effort was made; a tunnel was started in the rear of the cook-room mentioned above, intended to strike a small sewer which started from the south-east corner, and passing through the outer wall to the large sewer in front.

FAILURES. 61

Some sixteen or eighteen feet brought the tunnel under a brick furnace, in which were built several large kettles used in making soup for prisoners. This partially caved in, and fear of discovery caused this route to be abandoned.

With a determination to succeed, which no difficulty could weaken or disappointment overcome, another attempt, far more difficult than the preceding, was made. A portion of the stone floor of the cook-room was taken up, and the place supplied by a neatly-fitting board, which could be easily removed; and through this the working party descended every night. The plan was to escape by the sewer leading from the kitchen, but it was not large enough for a man to pass through; but as the route seemed preferable to any other, it was determined to remove the plank with which it was lined; and this out of the way, the tunnel or aperture would be sufficiently large. The old knives and saws were called for, and the work of removing the plank was continued for several days with flattering success, till it was concluded that another hour's work would enable us to enter the large sewer in front, into which this led, and thus escape. So strong was the conviction that the work would be completed in a little time, that all who knew the work was going on made preparation to escape on the night of the 26th of January. After working on the night of the 25th, two men were left down in the cellar to cover up all traces of the work during the day, and as soon as it was dark to complete the work—to go into the large sewer, explore it, and have every thing ready by eight or nine o'clock, at which time the bricks would be removed from the hole leading into the cellar, which had to be placed carefully in their original position every night, from the beginning to the completion of the work. When the last brick was removed, a rope-ladder, which had been prepared for the occasion, was passed down and made fast to a bar of iron, placed across the front of the fireplace. Now came long moments of breathless silence and agonizing suspense, all waiting for the assurance from one of the men below that all was ready. He came at last; but, alas! his first whisper was, "bad news, bad news;" and bad news, indeed, it proved. It was found that the remaining portion of the plank to be removed was oak, two inches thick, and impossible to be removed by the tools which had heretofore been used; moreover, the water was rapidly finding its way into the tunnel, and all the labor expended had been in vain. The feelings of that little band who can describe!—from hopes almost as bright as reality they were suddenly plunged into the depths of despair.

Nearly all the work above mentioned was performed by Captains Hamilton and Gallagher, Maj. Fitzsimmons, and another officer. As a natural consequence, they were worn-out by excessive labor, anxiety, and loss of sleep, that being the thirty-ninth night of unremitting toil.

They were, however, still unconquered in spirit, and declared that another attempt must be made as soon as they were sufficiently recruited to enter upon it. Noble fellows! hard had they toiled for liberty, and it came at last.

CHAPTER V.

THE TUNNEL.

A new plan adopted—Nature of the task—In the tunnel—Maj. M'Donald's adventure—My own disappearance—Given up as escaped—Fislar's story.

WHILE the party last named were resting, there were others not inactive. Capt. Clark, of the Seventy-Third Illinois, Maj. M'Donald, of the One Hundredth Ohio, Capt. Lucas, of the Fifth Kentucky, Lieut. Fislar, of the Seventh Indiana Battery, and myself, proposed to the originators of the plan of escape, that we would commence at some other point, and push on the work till they were sufficiently recruited to unite with us. This meeting with their approval, on the following night Maj. M'Donald and Capt. Clark went down and commenced operations.

The plan was to begin a new tunnel in the cellar on the east side, near the north-east corner of the building. The first thing to be done was to make a hole through the brick wall, which they effected in one day and night. This was done by picking the cement from between the bricks with a penknife, and then breaking them out with an old ax. This, of course, made considerable noise, and was calculated to arrest the attention of the guards; but it happened, providentially, as it seemed to us, that just at that time the authorities of the prison determined to place iron grates in all the windows, to render the escape of the Yankees impossible. This was accompanied by great noise; and while they were thus engaged our boys thumped away with a will, and made their way through the wall without exciting the least suspicion. The night after the breach was made, Lieut. Fislar and myself went down to work; but having nothing but a small penknife, our progress was, of necessity, very slow. In spite of all difficulties, however, we made an excavation of about two feet, and felt that we were that much nearer freedom. We remained in the cellar all the next day, and at night were relieved by two others; and thus the work was continued from night to night, till its completion. One of our number remained in the cellar every day to remove all signs of the previous night's work, and to replace the bricks in the cavity made in the wall, to avoid discovery, as some of the prison officials or laborers came into the cellar every day, either bringing in or taking out forage or commissary stores.

I have been asked a thousand times how we contrived to hide such a quantity of earth as the digging of a tunnel of that size would dislodge. There was a large pile of straw stored in the cellar for hospital use; in this we made a wide and deep opening, extending to the ground; in this the loose dirt was closely packed, and then nicely covered with straw.

As the work progressed from night to night, and our hopes increased with the length of our tunnel, the number of laborers was increased, till the working party numbered fourteen. This was the more necessary, as the work of removing the loose dirt increased with every foot we advanced. I have often been asked how we managed to get the dirt out of the tunnel, which was too narrow to permit a man to turn round in it. As the whole process was somewhat novel, one in all probability never attempted before, I will describe it for the benefit of the readers.

Our dirt-car was a wooden spittoon, with holes through each end opposite each other, through which ropes were passed; one of these ropes was used by the one engaged in digging, to draw the empty spittoon from the entrance to the place where he was at work; and when he had loosened earth enough to fill it, he gave a signal to the one at the mouth of the tunnel by jerking the rope, and he drew the loaded box out, and the miner recovered it by pulling the rope attached to the end of the box nearest him; thus it was kept traveling backward and forward till wagon-loads of earth were removed. After penetrating some distance the task became very painful; it was impossible to breathe the air of the tunnel for many minutes together; the miner, however, would dig as long as his strength would allow, or till his candle was extinguished by the foul air; he would then make his way out, and another would take his place—a place narrow, dark, and damp, and more like a grave than any place can be short of a man's last narrow home. As the work approached completion the difficulty of breathing in the tunnel was greatly increased, and four persons were necessary to keep the work moving; one would go in and dig awhile, then when he came out nearly exhausted another would enter and fill the spittoon, a third would draw it to the mouth of the tunnel, a fourth would then empty the contents into a large box provided for the purpose, and when it was full, take it to the straw pile and carefully conceal it, as before stated. This labor, too, it must be remembered, was not only extremely difficult in itself, and especially so when the imperfect tools and means of removing the earth are taken into the account; but in addition to this was the constant anxiety lest the attempt we were making should be discovered. Moreover, the fact that all previous attempts had failed was calculated at times to fill our minds with fears lest some unforeseen obstacle should occur to prevent the success of our enterprise. On the other hand, however, the hard fare and confinement of our prison, the monotony of which had become unendurable, and the possibility of escape at last roused us up to exertions almost superhuman. Under any other circumstances the work would have been deemed impossible; but there are no impossibilities to men with liberty as the result of their labors. Before the work was completed, those who had been engaged in the previous attempt had recovered from their exhaustion, and were able to take part in this, which, in the end, proved successful. But what is to be most regretted is, that though all of them regained the liberty for which they so patiently toiled, one of them was recaptured—the one, too, who, of all others, the rest confidently believed would escape, if escape were in the power of man. What he has since suffered we can only conjecture; but the disappointment must have been most sad to his great heart—to have gained the free air, and almost in sight of the flag of the Union—to be recaptured and borne back to a captivity more hopeless than before.

I have also been asked frequently since my escape, how it was possible for a man to be left down in the cellar every day without being discovered. Such a thing seems strange; but the entire work was a marvelous one, and this was a necessary part of it; and though the officers, or other persons employed about the prison, visited the cellar every day, yet for fifty-one days one or another of our company was down there without being discovered. The duty of the one left there was to remove all traces of the work of the previous night, as soon as it became light enough to do so; he would then conceal himself for the day in the straw, of which there was a large quantity there, and but for which our undertaking must have been discovered nearly as soon as begun. To account for the absence of those persons required some ingenuity, as two of our number were sometimes on duty at once in the cellar. This was managed as follows: the officers were drawn up in four ranks, and the clerk counted them from right to left; one, two, or three, as the case might be, would change their places so as to be counted twice; the number being all right, the clerk was deceived.

This, however, was suddenly brought to an end. Some of the officers had succeeded in obtaining citizens' clothes, and passed the guards without suspicion and escaped; one or two also escaped by disguising themselves in the Confederate uniform. After this we were all collected into the two east rooms, and required to answer to our names.

About the time the change was made Major M'Donald and Lieut. M'Kee were on duty in the cellar, and failed to answer to their names; this caused quite a stir, and for some time it was thought that they had escaped by a trick similar to that of the others. The next day they were reported by some one as being present—perhaps the clerk, who knew that the Major, particularly, would bear watching. The consequence was they were both called down to the office to render to Maj. Turner the reasons for their absence on the previous day. The Lieutenant, with an air of perfect innocence, stated that, feeling quite unwell, he had wrapped himself up in his blanket, had fallen asleep, did not hear the order for roll-call, and was overlooked. His excuse was deemed valid, and he was immediately sent back to his quarters. The Major was not so fortunate; the fact is, he was regarded as a suspicious character, and in consequence had a severer ordeal to pass. The question, "Major, your reason for non-attendance at roll-call yesterday," was put quite laconically. Said he, "I happened to be in Col. Streight's room, and failed to get back in time."

"In Col. Streight's room, indeed! How did you get in there, sir?"

That I may be understood better, it is necessary to state that some time previous some of the officers of Col. Streight's command had given much trouble to the authorities of the prison, by being in our room at roll-call; and, in order to prevent a similar occurrence, had nailed up the door between the rooms occupied by the Chickamauga officers, and those captured with Col. Streight. The door had not been nailed up half an hour before some quick-witted fellow sawed the door completely in two below the lock, extracted the nails, placed some benches near the door so as to conceal the crack, and we were thus able to pass in and out at pleasure. The occupants of the other room took good care that the traces of the saw should be concealed on their side, and thus free intercourse was kept between both rooms without being suspected.

The Major, with great seeming candor, explained the trick which accounted for his presence in the forbidden room; and the next question was, "How did it happen that the officer of the day and the clerk did not see you there when they came in to see if that room was cleared before commencing to call the roll?" This would have been a poser to many—not so to the Major, who readily replied, that, being in the wrong room, not wishing to be found there, and being compelled to disclose the means by which he entered, he had climbed up on the plate or girder that passed through the room;

"and when the search for me began," said he, "I laid there close to the timber for ten hours, and would have melted, drop by drop, before I would discover myself, and subject the officers in that room to censure, and cause all intercourse between the two rooms to be cut off."

His questioners seemed rather to doubt his excuse, ingenious though it was; but as they were ignorant of the true state of the case, and he reaffirmed his story so positively, he was dismissed to his quarters with a reprimand and an admonition.

The day after this occurred it was my turn to stand guard in the cellar. At quite an early hour the roll was called, and there being no one willing to run the risk of answering for me, my absence was discovered. There were several, it is true, who would willingly have answered for me, but they were so well known, and somewhat suspected, which would have rendered it dangerous to them, and of no benefit to me. The fact of my absence made it necessary for the calling of the roll several times in succession; all the officers were kept in rank, confined in one room, till three o'clock in the afternoon, and diligent search was made for me in every room in the building; and it was finally concluded that I had made my escape. At night, when the working party came down, they informed me of what had taken place; and upon consultation it was thought best that I should remain down in the cellar till the tunnel was completed. To remain in this cold, dark, and loathsome place was most revolting to my feelings; but the fear of being handcuffed and put in the dungeon if I returned to my room, and the hope of gaining my liberty shortly, induced me to stay. After agreeing to stay down, it was suggested that I might with safety go up to my quarters after lights were out, and sleep till four o'clock in the morning, and go down again when the working party came up. I did so; but the first night I was seen, either by some traitor, or very careless prisoner, not acquainted with our secret, who stated at roll-call the next morning, that I was in the house, as he had seen me go to bed the night before—which was really the case. The result was that the roll was called several times, and another careful search for me was instituted. Great excitement prevailed through the prison; those of our own men who knew nothing of the plan of escape, and the place of my concealment, thought that I was hiding in some of the rooms, and thought it very wrong in me to do so; they even said that I ought to come out of my hiding-place and give myself up, as they, though innocent, were suffering on my account. On the contrary, those who knew where I was declared that it was impossible that I could be in the building, after the strict search that had been made for me; and as others were known to have made their escape recently, it was more than likely that I had done the same.

This was corroborated by Lieut. Fislar, who improvised a story to fit the case. He said that he was my messmate and sleeping-companion—which was true; but that I had been missing from my usual place for some time, and he had no doubt but that I had escaped. He said, moreover, that two of my cousins were among our guards—that I had been courting their favor for some time, and that they had finally furnished me with a rebel uniform—that I had made a wooden sword, a tin scabbard, and a belt out of a piece of oil-cloth, and that they had eventually passed me out as a rebel officer.

This story was taken up and so stoutly confirmed by all who knew where I was, that the point was yielded by most of the opposite view, though a few still contended that I must be in the prison still.

All this was related to me by the working party when they came down at night, and I then resolved to make my appearance at my quarters no more. This resolution I have kept faithfully. I never saw my room again, and never desire to do so, unless it be as the bearer of freedom to those who are pining there still.

CHAPTER VI.

CELLAR LIFE.

My home and company—Great alarm—Still safe—The work renewed—Success—The last night in Libby—Words on leaving.

THE cellar was now my home. I was fed by my companions, who nightly brought me down a portion of their own scanty fare. Had I been discovered by the authorities of the prison it would have gone hard with me; and knowing this, the greatest sympathy was manifested by my associates, who felt that this danger was incurred not less for their advantage than my own.

Every thing moved on as well as could be expected. I had plenty of company—little of it, however, agreeable, as it consisted of rebels, rats, and other vermin. With the former I had no communication whatever; whenever they made their appearance I leaped quickly into a hole I had prepared in the straw, and pulled the hole in after me, or nearly so, at least, by drawing the straw over me so thickly that I could scarcely breathe. The rats gave me no annoyance, save when making more noise than usual, they startled me by making the impression that my two-legged enemies were near; the remaining nuisance, which shall be nameless, was one which all prisoners will ever remember with loathing, and from which there was neither respite nor escape.

The night of the seventh of February came, and it was thought that our tunnel was long enough to reach the inside of a tobacco-shed on the opposite side of the street, under which it passed. We made our calculation in the following manner: Captain Gallagher had obtained permission to go to a building across the street, where the boxes sent from the North to the prisoners were stored, to obtain some of the perishable articles; and while crossing the street he measured the distance, as accurately as possible, by stepping it both ways, and came to the conclusion that fifty-two or fifty-three feet would bring us to the shed. On measuring the tunnel it was found to be fifty-three feet long, and we fondly hoped that our labors were ended, with the exception of a few feet upward to the light. So confident were we that the work could be completed in an hour or two, that we had our rations already prepared in our haversacks, fully expecting to begin going out at nine o'clock—nay, we even went so far as to communicate the success of our plan to many who had not been partakers in the labor or the secret of the undertaking, but whom we invited to become the companions of our flight. When all were thus expectant, all thinking that the long-wished-for hour had come, Capt. Randall, of the Second Ohio, was appointed to open up the way to light and liberty.

It was agreed that the mining party, who had labored so faithfully, should go out first, and that our friends should follow; and we stood anxiously awaiting the return of Capt. Randell, with the news that the way was open. There are times when minutes seem lengthened into hours—this was one of them. The suspense began to be painful; it seemed as if we could hear the beatings of each other's hearts, as well as feel the throbbings of our own, and the unspoken question on every lip was, Will he succeed? At length he emerged from the tunnel, and, in answer to the question, "What success?" in an excited tone and manner he replied, "All is lost!" We gathered round him, and when he became somewhat calmer he spoke as follows: "I have made an opening, but a large stone which lay on the surface fell into the tunnel, making considerable noise; the hole, too, was on the outside of the shed, and within a few feet of the sentinel who was on guard; he heard the noise, and called the attention of the other sentinel to it; the light from the hospital shone upon the side of the shed; I could see both the guards walking toward the spot; I have no doubt they have discovered the tunnel, and perhaps will soon be in here to arrest us."

Imagine, if you can, our feelings; our bright hopes so suddenly crushed, and every one in expectation that the guard would soon be upon us. Great excitement prevailed, yet no one was able to suggest how to act in this sudden and unexpected emergency.

Amid all the excitement, however, incident to such an occasion, there was much sympathy felt in my behalf. I had been missing for some time, and was supposed to have made my escape; to be discovered now, as seemed inevitable, would be proof that I had much to do with the attempt to escape, and would subject me, at the very least, to the dungeon and handcuffs. In a few moments the cellar was nearly cleared, most of the party returning to their quarters in the different rooms above; but Maj. M'Donald and Capt. Hamilton remained with me, determined, if they could not aid me, at least to share the same fate. Noble, self-sacrificing men! their conduct proved that disinterested friendship and high, chivalrous feeling have not yet departed.

After all was quiet the Major determined to go up stairs and make what discoveries he could. He soon returned, saying he had been up to the upper east room, from which he could see the sentinels very distinctly; and, from all appearances, he concluded that they had not discovered the hole. I advised him to go into the tunnel and examine the breach, and stop it up if possible, as it was not at the right place to render our escape at all likely, being outside of the shed instead of inside, as was intended, and within a few feet of the guard. If the hole could not be stopped, of course it exposed us to certain discovery in the morning; and I proposed to go in and enlarge it, and, great as was the risk, try to make my escape at all hazards; for if I should fail, I would rather be caught in the attempt than wait to be found in the cellar or my quarters. When the Major returned he reported favorably, saying that the breach might be repaired. An old pair of pantaloons were procured and stuffed full of earth; some dirt, too, was put on the outside of them, so that the cloth could not be seen, and thus excite suspicion. These were forced into the aperture, and earth pressed in beneath; and he returned greatly elated with the hope that all danger was past, and that in one or two more nights our labors would be crowned with success.

After a few minutes' consultation it was agreed that I should remain in the cellar till the next night. All the next day a close watch was kept, by some of our number in the east room, on the guards who were stationed near the place where our tunnel ended. There was no token, however, that any discovery had been made, and the next night the mining operations were resumed, and between two and three o'clock in the morning an opening was made to the free air, this time inside of the shed, at the very point we desired, at a distance of fifty-seven feet from the point of starting. The tunnel was about two feet wide by two feet and a half deep; it was arched above; and Lieut. Davy, who is a practical miner, declared that it was done in a workmanlike manner. We found a very hard, compact sand all the route; the loose earth was disposed of as I have before stated, till within about ten feet of the end, when it was strewn along the entire length, thus reducing very considerably the size of the passage. Near the terminus it was rather a close fit for a large man, and when I was passing through I stuck fast, and had to call on Maj. Fitzsimmons to pull me out of a very tight place.

The principal tool used in this work was a chisel, which was found among some rubbish in the cellar, a handle for which was made from a piece of stove-wood.

When the surface was reached there was too little of the night remaining to effect our escape; two of our number, however, passed out and explored the lot, and planned the course to be taken after emerging from the tunnel. The shed in which our labors terminated fronted the canal; between them was a brick building, through the center of which there was a passage into the lot, closed by a gate; and the route fixed upon was through this passage. The question then arose, who shall go out first? Some thought that I was entitled to that honor, as I had been confined so long in the cellar, and had incurred more risk than the rest. Others thought that, though to go out first might be esteemed the post of honor, it was also the post of danger, as the first would run more risk than those who should follow. It was finally agreed that I should be the fifth to pass out, and that Lieut. Fislar should be my partner in flight. Then arose the question, how the aperture through the surface should be concealed till the next night; for should any one go into the shed during the day, as was most probable, our plan might yet be frustrated. A piece of plank was found, and Capt. Hamilton dispatched with it to the outer end of the tunnel, over which he placed it, being careful, however, to bury it just below the surface, and to cover it with dry earth. He soon returned, having successfully accomplished his task; and all retired to their quarters, leaving me in the cellar to cover up all traces of their work—cheered by the thought that with night would come liberty.

The ninth of February was a long day, and long to be remembered; never was my anxiety so great as for the setting of that day's sun; and more than once during its long, dreary hours I feared that the cup of happiness, now so near our lips, would be rudely dashed away. Business often brought those connected with the prison into the cellar, as it contained articles constantly needed; but on that day it was visited much oftener than usual. One party brought a dog in with them, and hissed him after the rats; and in his search after them he passed over and around me, and every moment I expected to be drawn from my place of concealment; but I was too large game for him, and I escaped. Soon after a rebel sergeant came in, with some negroes, after some empty barrels that were stowed in the back part of the cellar. In one of the barrels they found a haversack full of provisions, left there by one of our party the preceding night. This I thought would certainly awaken suspicion, and give rise to a strict search; the negroes, however, took the food and ate it, without the question being raised how it came there. But the danger had not yet passed; for, in carrying out the barrels, one of the negroes stepped over my feet, almost touching them. Night came at length, and never was sunlight hailed more gladly than darkness, for it brought an end to our fears and captivity.

The path to freedom is now open; but pardon me, kind reader, if I delay a moment on the threshold, as it were, of a prison that I trust soon to leave forever, to look over the sad hours spent in its walls, and the methods taken by its inmates to make the hours seem less weary. Much of my own time, and that of my fellow-laborers, was so taken up with our project, that we suffered less than the great body of prisoners, whose time and thoughts were not thus occupied. To them the routine of prison life became intolerably oppressive, and every device was employed to pass away the long, long hours. Books and fragments of books were eagerly devoured; newspapers were read till they would scarcely hold together. At times shouts of uproarious laughter would be heard; and a casual observer would have thought that a more careless, light-hearted band could not be found; but, alas! much of the laughter rang above a sad heart; and to those who knew the thoughts of those so outwardly gay, there was something in that laughter sadder far than tears. Many were anxiously exercised upon the questions, what shall we eat? what shall we drink? and wherewithal shall we be clothed? but their solicitude never led them to a satisfactory conclusion. Others would go through the forms of fashionable life, and invitations to parties, and to dine, were frequent; but the rich viands and sparkling wines, like those of the banquet recorded in the Arabian Nights, existed only in the imagination of the guests.

Wealth is only a relative term at last. He was well-off in Libby who had two pewter spoons, an extra tin cup or plate; rich who possessed a ham and a box of crackers—a millionaire if, in addition to these, he had a pound or two of tobacco. The silver ware in our wealthiest mansions is never looked after as carefully as were the extra spoons, forks, or plates, which a man or mess claimed; and when they disappeared, as they sometimes would, as much skill and craft would be employed to recover them as a corps of detectives would display when a bank has been robbed, or a palace plundered. Many pined away with melancholy, and the history of the hearts which have been crushed would be a sad one; many left us during my stay for the hospital—from thence it was not far to the grave. There were, however, stout hearts which would not yield to discouragement—men who never for a moment yielded to despair; they had faith in their Government, in the justice of the cause for which they were suffering, and, best of all, some of them had faith in God.

CHAPTER VII.

THE ESCAPE.

The last night—Farewell to Libby—Sufferings and dangers—The north star our guide—The faithful negro—A false friend—Almost retaken—The contrast.

IT came at last—the last night, the night of release; and the working party was assembled in the cellar for the last time. There was a shade of sadness on many a brow; for we were about to go forth two by two, to separate to meet again—when? Perhaps never! The party consisted of

    COL. ROSE, 77th Pennsylvania Infantry.
    MAJ. FITZSIMMONS, 30th Indiana Infantry.
    CAPT. HAMILTON, 12th Kentucky Cavalry.
    CAPT. GALLAGHER, 2d Ohio Volunteer Infantry.
    CAPT. CLARK, 79th Illinois Vol. Infantry.
    CAPT. LUCAS, 5th Kentucky Vol. Infantry.
    MAJ. M'DONALD, 100th Ohio Vol. Infantry.

CAPT. RANDELL, 2d Ohio Vol. Infantry.
CAPT. I. N. JOHNSTON, 6th Ky. Vol. Infantry.
LIEUT. FISLAR, 7th Indiana Battery.
LIEUT. SIMPSON, 10th Indiana Infantry.
LIEUT. MITCHELL, 79th Illinois Infantry.
LIEUT. DAVY, 77th Pennsylvania Infantry.
LIEUT. STERLING, 29th Indiana Infantry.
LIEUT. FOSTER, 30th Indiana Infantry.

It was agreed that ten minutes should elapse after the first two passed out, before the second couple should start. Lieut. Fislar and myself were the third couple. After emerging from the tunnel we faced to the right, and passed across the lot to the passage through the brick building, already described, into the street; and in doing so we passed within forty feet of the sentinels. We were not observed, and you may be sure we did not linger, and soon we were out of sight of the hated place.

One hundred and nine persons thus escaped from eight o'clock at night to three in the morning, notwithstanding that the night was clear and beautiful, and all had to pass between two gas lights; of these, however, only about one half succeeded in reaching the Federal lines.

As my comrade and myself were passing through the city, two ladies, who were standing at the gate of a house which stood back from the street, observed us; one of them remarked to the other that we looked like Yankees. We did not stop to undeceive them, and met with no further trouble till the city limits were passed. We then changed our course and traveled northeast, and soon came to the rebel camps, which stretched round a great portion of the city. We were excited, of course, and bewildered for the first hour, not knowing whether we were in the path of safety or danger. All at once I became perfectly composed, and told my comrade to follow me and I would conduct him safe through. I then started due north, taking the north star for my guide, changing my course only when we came near any of the camps, sufficiently to avoid them. After traveling three or four miles we saw another camp ahead, and thinking that the camps possibly did not connect, we determined to attempt to pass between them. As we approached, however, we found out our mistake—the camps were connected by a chain of sentinels, and this chain must be passed before escape became even probable.

We advanced cautiously, and when we reached a small ravine we could hear the sentinel, on his beat, on the other side. We saw his fire, too, which we, of course, avoided; and at one time only a few small bushes were between us and the guard; the wind, however, was blowing briskly, causing quite a rustling among the dry leaves, and we succeeded in getting by safely. We moved on rapidly, and soon came near the cavalry pickets; these we passed without difficulty. After continuing our course north for some time, we changed to north-east, and passed over four lines of the rebel defenses. It was our intention to strike the Chickahominy above the railroad bridge; but, to our surprise, we struck the railroad on the Richmond side.

We then traveled down the road about a mile, and as day began to dawn we left the road a short distance to find a hiding-place, expecting that with the coming of light there would be a keen search made for us. The rebel fortifications were near; in front of them all the timber had been felled, and among this timber was our hiding-place the first day—all the safer, too, no doubt, for being within a few hundred yards of the rebel guns. The weather was excessively cold; we had walked during the night over bad roads, through mud and water, and our pantaloons were frozen stiff up to our knees. We did not dare to make a fire so near the rebel camp, for fear of discovery; but our suffering was greatly lessened by the thought that we were free.

As soon as it was light enough to see, we made the rather unpleasant discovery that there was a picket-guard not more than one hundred and fifty yards from the place where we had taken refuge; and soon two working parties came out from the fortifications, and began to cut cord-wood. These two parties, with the picket-guard, formed a triangle — the woodchoppers on each side, the guards in front; so that we were obliged, half frozen though we were, to lay very close to the ground till kind and merciful Night, who kindly lends her mantle to escaped prisoners, should come.

This, the first day of our escape, was a long one, full of anxiety and fears, lest, after all our toils, we should be retaken and subjected to a captivity far worse than we had experienced before. About sundown the working party withdrew, and soon after nightfall we resumed our journey, again toward the north star. We had scarcely got fairly started before our ears were saluted by the tramp of horses and the clank of sabers; we immediately left the road and lay down behind some brushwood. It proved to be a scouting party, perhaps in pursuit of us; but we let them pass unchallenged. We continued our course till we reached the

Chickahominy River; going up the stream a short distance we found a log across it, passed over and kept our course for several miles, then changed our course north-east, and traveled till nearly daylight. We camped for the day by the side of a swamp, under a large pine-tree, near the foot of which was a thick cedar bush, whose shade we found most welcome, as it afforded us concealment and shelter from the bleak wind. The night had been very cold, and having crossed several swamps in our journey, our feet were wet, and our clothes frozen, as, indeed, was the case, day and night, till we reached the Union lines. During the night we were able to keep the blood in circulation by active exercise; but being compelled to lie still during the day for fear of discovery, we came very near perishing from cold. That day I thought our feet certainly would freeze; and as necessity will often set the wits to work, I fell upon an expedient which doubtless saved us from such a disaster.

Before leaving the prison I had taken the precaution to put on two shirts—one of them a woolen one; this I pulled off; and having taken off our shoes and socks, we lay down close together, and rolled our feet up in it, and found great relief. About noon some cows came around us; and as the spot was a sheltered one, they seemed inclined to remain. Fearing that some one would soon be in search of them, we got up and drove them away; and very soon a woman came, evidently looking for them. We lay very close to the ground as long as she was in sight, and breathed more freely when she disappeared. A celebrated traveler says that he was invariably well treated by women in the various countries through which he traveled; much as we regard the sex, we fear that it would be a dangerous experiment for an escaped prisoner to trust even the gentlest and fairest in rebeldom.

On the night of the eleventh we traveled east, and crossed the railroad about half-past eight o'clock; we also crossed the main road from Richmond to Williamsburg, and two or three other roads, all leading into the main road from the Chickahominy, and just before day went into a hiding-place near one of these roads. As soon as it was light we saw that our place of rest was not well chosen; that scouts, or any one in pursuit of us, could come close upon us before we could see them; we therefore sought another place, from which we could see to a considerable distance in every direction. We then pulled off our shoes and socks, and wrapped our feet up in the flannel shirt, as before, and endeavored to get a little sleep. It was so cold, however, that we could sleep but little, and then never both at once; we were still in such danger that one would watch while the other rested. Sometimes in our night marches we would become so tired and sleepy that we would throw ourselves down on the ground and sleep a short time, till awakened by the excessive cold, and then rise and walk briskly till our chilled blood began to move faster in its channels.

We were careful to shun every thing in the shape of a man, whether black or white; but after traveling through swamps and thickets, on the fourth night we came to a path along which a negro man was passing; we stopped him and asked a number of questions, and were convinced, from his answers, that he was a friend, and might be trusted. We then told him our condition, and asked him if he could give us something to eat. He said that he was not near home, or he would do so cheerfully; but pointing to a house in the distance, to which he said he was going, assured us that friends lived there, and if we would go with him our wants should be supplied. He said the people who lived there were Union folks, and that we need not fear; but we had suffered so much that we did not feel inclined to trust strangers; however, I asked him to go to the house and see if any rebel soldiers were there. This he did readily, and soon returned, telling us to come on, that the way was clear, and supper, such as they had, would soon be prepared for us. I then asked him if he would stand guard while we went in, as I was still fearful of being retaken. He agreed to do so. We then entered the house, found a good fire, and some friendly faces; and the inmates set about preparing supper for us with all speed. We happened to have a little coffee with us, the very thing of which they seemed most in need. We added this to their store, and soon we had the first good meal we had taken for months before us, and a cheery cup of hot coffee, which made it seem a feast. After the meal was ended, being fully satisfied that the people were friends, and our black friend outside faithful, we rested awhile, which we certainly needed, if ever men did, and gave to our kind entertainers all that we could—our heart-felt thanks. When we were ready to start, the faithful negro sentinel, who had stood guard for us, offered to be our guide, and conducted us about four miles on our journey; he advised us to cross to the north side of the road, as we should meet with fewer swamps, and consequently make better progress. He added other directions which we found to be valuable, and we never shall forget the kindness of the warm heart which beat in that black man's breast.

We then traveled on till daylight, and stopped, as usual, for the day; but our clothes were so wet and frozen that we were obliged to travel on to keep from being perfectly benumbed with cold. We had not traveled any in the daytime before, and began to think that we were out of danger; still, we kept a vigilant watch, but met with no interruption, and we gradually became bolder. About sundown we saw before us a negro chopping wood; and as he was directly in our line of march, and our adventure of the previous night had given us confidence in those having black skins, we walked directly toward him, intending to inquire about the roads, the position of the rebel pickets, the movements of scouting parties, and other matters of interest. Judge of our surprise, however, when we came within a few paces of him, to find a white man with him, seated at the foot of a tree! It was too late to change our course, as he evidently saw us; so we went up to him and inquired how far it was to Barnesville, a small town we had passed a few miles back. He answered us civilly, and we asked several other questions, which he replied to satisfactorily. He gave us to understand, however, that he recognized us as Union soldiers. We told him that was not the case, but that we were Confederate scouts in disguise, and asked him if he had, during the past few days, seen any Yankees in that vicinity. He said that he had not, and insisted that we were Federal soldiers ourselves. At length I told him we were, and that we had escaped from Libby Prison. He protested that he was glad to see us, had heard of the escape of the Libby prisoners, but did not credit it—but must believe it now, as he had the living witnesses before him. He talked freely with us, saying, among other things, that he was a citizen, and had taken no part whatever in the war, and even expressed the wish that we might make our escape. I told him that I expected, as soon as we were gone, that he would go to the nearest picket-post and inform his rebel friends what course we had taken. He declared that he had no such intention, and repeated the wish that we might have a safe journey. I then asked him if he knew of any pickets near. He replied there were none nearer than Burnt Ordinary, which was some miles distant, and that he had not seen a Confederate soldier for three weeks—in fact, that they seldom came in that direction. The truth was, as we soon discovered, there was a picket-post not more than half a mile from the place where we stood. This he well knew, and did his utmost to betray us into their hands. He advised us to follow a certain path, by doing which he said we should avoid a swamp that it was difficult and dangerous to cross, and even went with us a short distance to see that we did not take the wrong path. I could not, however, resist the conviction that he was treacherous, and did all I could to impress him with a salutary fear, telling him that if he informed on us, there was a certain Gen. Butler, of whom he had doubtless heard, who had a way of finding such things out; and if any thing happened to us he would doubtless send out a detachment that would destroy every thing that he had. If, however, he conducted himself as a quiet, peaceable citizen, he and his property would be respected. He assured us that no harm should come to us through him, shook hands with us, and wished us again a safe journey.

We had not gone over a hundred yards, when happening to look back, I saw our friend traveling at a pace quite unnecessary for one so friendly, and the whole matter flashed on my mind. I turned to my comrade and said, "We are gone up; that scoundrel, I feel certain, has gone to report us to the nearest picket-guard!"

So well assured did I feel of his treachery, that I proposed that we should change our course from south to east, which we did immediately—and then almost too late. We had not pursued our new course more than half a mile when we heard voices of men talking in a low yet earnest tone; we stopped and listened; it was even as I had suspected—the professed friend, from whom we had recently parted, had gone to the nearest pickets, informed the rebels who we were, and how we might be intercepted; and the officer was now placing his men on the road near where we were expected to cross, and we were now within fifteen or twenty paces of them—they, aware of our coming, wary and watchful. It was a moment of fearful suspense; we were screened from view, however, by the bushes; and our only chance was to change our course; we started, but the rustling of the dry leaves beneath our feet betrayed us, and we were sternly ordered to come out of the brush. We hesitated, and the order was repeated in fierce, quick tones, which was accompanied by a volley of musketry. On this we came out at a double-quick, but in a direction opposite to that which we were thus rudely invited—in other words, we broke away and ran for life. With a shout our enemies joined in the pursuit, and pressed us so closely that I was obliged to throw away my overcoat, and Lieut. Fislar lost his cap. On came our pursuers, nearer and nearer, till, at length, in order to save ourselves, we had to take refuge in a large swamp. Orders were given to surround it, and we could hear men on every side calling to each other, and giving direction how to prevent our escape—and all this when liberty was almost in our grasp; for we were then but three miles from the Federal lines.

While thus lying concealed in the swamp our reflections were not of the most agreeable character. We had almost reached the reward of much toil and suffering; we had even begun to think and talk of home and the loved ones there; and now, by the baseness of one of our fellow-beings, to lose the prize almost in our grasp, was too painful a thought to be calmly endured. We contrasted the duplicity—nay, almost perjury, of the civilized white man who had betrayed us into the power of our enemies, with the fidelity of the African slave who had proved so kind and true, and felt that under the dark skin beat the nobler heart. The one, of our own race, in violation of promises the most solemn, would have given us back to a fate worse than death; the other, of another and despised race, did all in his power to restore us to freedom and home.

CHAPTER VIII.

UNDER THE FLAG AGAIN.

In the swamp—Meeting our pickets—Warm welcome—Aid to the fugitives—Kind treatment—Interview with Gen. Butler—Arrival at Washington.

THUS encircled by our enemies, our only hope of escape lay in crossing the swamp in front of us, which was a most perilous undertaking, as all who have any acquaintance with the swamps of the Chickahominy well know. The remembrance of the prison we had left, and the fear of one even worse if retaken, urged us on; and, after many difficulties, our efforts were at last successful. We attempted to cross four or five times before we were able to do so, and more than once we were ready to despair. In one of our attempts I stepped from a log and went down into mud waist-deep; every motion I made only served to carry me down still lower; but my true friend Fislar was at hand, and saved me from a horrible fate. He came to the end of the log, and I roused every energy and threw myself toward him; he was just able to reach my hand, which was eagerly stretched out to him, and he drew me exhausted from the mire.

Never can I forget that kind, generous friend—a truer man to country and friends does not live; the trials through which we passed only served to develop his noble nature, and he will ever seem dear as a brother to me. He is a noble specimen of a man, physically; has dark hair, brown eyes, and light complexion—is six feet high, well-proportioned, and has an agreeable face—is possessed of fine natural abilities, is twenty-three years of age, brave, active, and daring, ready for any emergency— and, to crown all, has as noble a heart as ever beat in human breast; and, for friend and companion, at home or abroad, in prosperity or adversity, there is no one that I have ever known that I would prefer to him.

After I was thus rescued we sat down awhile to rest; and when somewhat refreshed made another attempt to cross. We found a place where a number of dead trees stood in the swamp, from which the branches had fallen; and by jumping from one to the other of these, and occasionally slipping into mud knee-deep, we reached the middle of the swamp; and in looking both before and behind us, it really seemed as if we were the first human beings who had ever penetrated to that dismal and solitary place. A stream, narrow, dark, and deep, now lay before us, and checked further progress; but the kind Providence which had aided us on so many occasions did not desert us now; for we found near the spot a slab that had been washed down from a saw-mill, which afforded us the means of crossing, and we were soon safely on the other side. Now that we were over the stream, a large portion of swamp had still to be traversed; but we felt that every step brought us nearer to friends and safety, so we plodded on cheerfully, and late at night struck the high ground on the other side.

Being exhausted by our journey through a swamp, which would have been deemed impassable had we not been urged on by hopes before and fears behind, we stopped for a time to gather strength for new efforts, hoping before sunrise to be beyond the reach of successful pursuit. Again we began our march, and near midnight we saw the picket-fires near Burnt Ordinary, but supposed them to be those of the rebels, as we had been told by the man who had betrayed us, that the rebels had a picket-guard at that place, which was true; but that evening, before we reached there, the Union cavalry had driven them away, and the fires we saw were those of our own pickets. Our narrow escape had rendered us very cautious; and having every reason to believe that the fires in sight were those of the enemy, we passed around them at what we thought a safe distance, and then struck out for Williamsburg, then, as we afterward learned, about twelve miles distant. We had not gone far before we were halted. Inquiring of the sentinel who he was, and where we were, he informed us that he belonged to the Eleventh Pennsylvania Cavalry, which was under Gen. Butler's command. As we had tried to play Confederate ourselves, we were not certain but that this might be one of them trying to play Yankee. After questioning him very closely, and being fully satisfied that he was "all right," we advanced. When we got up to him he told us that he and his comrades had been sent out on that advanced post in order to meet and aid prisoners who were said to have escaped from Libby Prison; and, added he, "I guess you are some of them." We told him we were, and he expressed great pleasure at meeting with us, and we felt what words never can express—a joy which can never be felt save by those who, after privations and anxieties like ours, feel that they are safe at last.

The sentinel then conducted us to the reserve-post, where we were warmly greeted, every one proffering aid in one way or another. After warming ourselves at the camp-fire, the officer in command, seeing our need of food and rest, proposed to send us on to the camp; and asked his men if any of them would furnish us with horses. "You can have mine! you can have mine!" was heard on every side, all seeming eager to help us; and soon we were well mounted, and on our way to the main body. We were conducted to Capt. Akerly's quarters, who gave us a hearty welcome; and though it was now after midnight, he soon had a good supper, with the luxurious addition of a cup of hot coffee, prepared for us, and congratulations on our good fortune poured in on all sides. After giving him a brief account of our trials, we informed him that it was reported through the country that the Federal pickets were advanced as far as Barnsville, which we now had learned was not the case; and we feared that some of our friends who had escaped might, on hearing this, venture in there and be recaptured. The Captain told us that he was about sending a company in that direction just before we got in—that they were now preparing to start, and he would have them keep a sharp lookout for our friends. Just then Lieut. Palmer reported to the Captain for orders, saying that the detachment was ready to move. The Captain put in his possession all that he had just learned from us; and he was about leaving, when my comrade, Lieut. Fislar, sprang up, asked to be furnished with a horse and saber, and to be permitted to accompany him in search of our companions, who were still subjected to the dangers which we had so narrowly escaped. His request was granted, and he was soon in the saddle and away.

This act was characteristic of the man;

and when it is remembered that he had been on the march near thirty hours, had just been hunted by the rebels like a pack of hounds in full cry, had just crossed a swamp which most men would have deemed madness to attempt, it must be regarded as noble and chivalrous in the highest degree. Most men, under similar circumstances, would eagerly have embraced the opportunity offered and needed for rest; but with a most unselfish devotion he forgot past dangers and present weariness, in his great desire for the safety of those, his former companions, who, cold, hungry, and half clad, were struggling still through forests and swamps to freedom.

The next morning, having been furnished with horse, sword, and pistol, I moved forward with the column, which was composed of picked men from three companies of the Eleventh Pennsylvania Cavalry. My position was in front with the Captain—every man with eager eyes on the look-out for the late inmates of Libby.

We had not advanced more than two miles before we saw two men emerge from a thicket and regard us anxiously; they were immediately recognized as escaped prisoners; but O, what emotions filled my heart when I saw and knew the well-known forms and faces of Maj. Fitzsimmons and Capt. Gallagher, of the old working party—companions in suffering, and soon to be partakers of joy such as mine! Spurring my horse in advance of the rest, and swinging my hat and cheering as I went, I hastened to meet my old companions — and seldom is so much joy pressed into a few brief moments as was ours when we met; we wept, we laughed, we shouted aloud in our joy, and warmer, gladder greetings will never be exchanged till we meet in the land where there are no partings. Our men came up and welcomed the fugitives warmly—not a man in the band who was not willing to dismount and let the wearied ones ride; and together we rode in search of others whom we doubted not were near; and during the day eleven more were added to our number—each one of them increasing our joy. I have known hours in my captivity when I have almost lost faith in man; but that day my faith in humanity was restored. To see those poor, hunted, suffering, wearied ones treated with all the tenderness and affection of brothers, by men whom they had never met till that hour, was sufficient to convince the most skeptical that earth yet abounds in warm, unselfish hearts. As we rode along we talked of our past trials, and the dangers we had passed since the night we parted in the cellar of Libby Prison, and speculated concerning the fate of others, whom we trusted would be as fortunate as ourselves, and to whom we would have borne aid, could we but have found them, at the risk of life itself.

During the day we had several skirmishes with the rebel scouts, and captured a few horses and accouterments, and returned the same evening to Williamsburg, when another detachment was sent out on a mission similar to that in which we had been engaged; and I need not say they bore with them our warmest wishes for their success.

With regard to the officers and men of the Eleventh Pennsylvania Cavalry, I can say, with truth, that they are the most daring, energetic, and enterprising men that I have met with since I have been in the service—the bravest of the brave; and the work which they fail in will be left undone. But this is not their highest praise—since I left my mother's care I have never felt so much like a baby as I have since I fell into their hands; nothing that could minister to the comfort of myself and comrades was left undone; they are as kind and tender as they are brave and true. God bless them, every one! The sutler of the regiment is worthy of special mention. When we reached our lines we were nearly all destitute of shoes and socks, and some even of other articles of clothing. Whatever we needed he readily furnished, and refused to receive any thing at our hands in return; but he can not refuse, I am sure, the heart-felt gratitude which will spring up in every one of our breasts at the recollection of the kindness shown by George M'Alpine.

During our stay at Williamsburg most of us remained with the Eleventh Pennsylvania— a few, however, were with the First New York Mounted Rifles; and they really seemed to strive to see which could treat us best. Our party had now increased to twenty-six—every new arrival was loudly and warmly greeted; the adventures of many of them were strange and stirring. May they live to tell their wondering grandchildren the story of their sufferings in Libby, and their marvelous escape!

We were all furnished with transportation to Yorktown. From thence we went by boat to Fortress Monroe, and were conducted by Gen. Wistar to head-quarters, and introduced to Gen. Butler, who expressed the greatest pleasure at our escape, and only regretted that some of our number had again fallen into the hands of the enemy. We had, of course, to go over the story of our treatment while in the hands of the rebels, and our perils on the way to the Union lines; and were made to feel the contrast by the attention bestowed upon us. Every heart seemed full of sympathy, and every tongue had a kind word. For ourselves, words were powerless to express the gratitude we felt for such constant kindness. The General ordered dinner to be prepared for our entire party, and authorized us to draw upon his quartermaster for any thing we needed; every wish seemed to be anticipated, every desire gratified—save one, the earnest longing for home. Even this was soon granted, by furnishing us transportation to Washington; from which place we started to our various homes; and O, how glad was our welcome! Many had mourned us as dead, and our return was like the grave giving up those it had once claimed as its own; and we were unutterably glad to be under the old flag and at home once more.

CHAPTER IX.

RETURN TO THE FRONT.

Return home—How I spent my furlough—Join my regiment—Changes—Forward movement—Tunnel Hill—Rocky Face—Resaca.

WITH the preceding chapter it was intended that my story should end; but in the judgment of others, whose opinions it would be improper to disregard, it was thought best that I should add a short sketch of Sherman's celebrated campaign, which resulted in the capture of Atlanta. The part taken by my regiment in this, one of the most arduous and successful enterprises of the war, is worthy of remembrance, and will be of no less interest to my brave companions in arms than the scenes already described; and being in actual command of the remnant of that noble band of men known as the Sixth Kentucky, whose deeds of daring in that memorable march should never be forgotten, my position gave me ample opportunity to know how uncomplainingly they bore the fatigue and privations of the march; how firmly they held the post of honor and danger; how gallantly they charged the foe, and how nobly they fell.

It is a sad thought, that many who entered the service with me in this regiment three years ago, will never read these lines; for they are sleeping in quiet, nameless graves, over which loved ones will never come to weep; their deeds and generous self-devotion to their country in her hour of peril shall never be forgotten; and sorrowing friends will take a melancholy pleasure, as they read these pages, in remembering that those whom they shall see on earth no more were not victims in a useless and wicked struggle, but martyrs, rather, in a cause for which it is glorious to die.

To resume, then, the thread of my narrative.

On reaching Washington our party was extremely anxious to visit their homes before again entering active service; and in order to do this furloughs and back pay were necessary. There was such a pressure of business at the War Office that we found great difficulty in having our wishes gratified in the particulars above named. At length, however, we found in Mr. Montfort, agent from Indiana to attend to the interests of the soldiers of that State, a friend whose sympathies were not bounded by the Ohio River, but one who was ever ready to aid all who wore the uniform of our common country. Our recent escape, and the dangers we had passed, enlisted his liveliest regard; and being familiar with the forms of business, he soon procured for us the desired furloughs, and the not less necessary pay. Nor did we confine our gratitude to empty expressions alone; before leaving for our homes we presented him with a very handsome testimonial in the shape of a beautiful cane, with gold head and appropriate inscription; and we feel greatly his debtors still, and trust that when declining years shall render necessary the staff to support his feeble steps, that his mind may be consoled by the reflection that his unselfish exertions on our behalf are gratefully cherished.

Home was now in immediate prospect; yet, so endeared had we become by association in Libby, and the perils attending our escape, that our parting was not without emotion. But soon there came to us all glad meetings—the embracings and welcomes of loved ones, and the cup of our joy was full. I made my way to Carrollton, Ky., the residence of my brother, the Rev. J. J. Johnston, and soon forgot the perils of the past in the joys of the present.

The days of my short furlough of thirty days passed rapidly; another of fifteen days was granted, and they, too, I need not say, passed sweetly and swiftly away; for in the first weeks of my home life I gave myself up to the delicious reveries of Love's young dream, and changed that dream only for the honeymoon, by giving my hand to Miss Annie Nash, in whose keeping my heart had long been.

Furloughs, however, like all things else on earth, have an end; and leaving friends—a nearer friend now than all the rest—my wife—behind, I hurried to the front, and joined my regiment between Knoxville and Chattanooga, a few days before the campaign against Atlanta began. My comrades gave me a hearty welcome; but there were faces that I missed, and well-known voices that I heard not—faces that I shall see and voices that I shall hear on earth no more. I had been spared amid all the dangers and sufferings of captivity; but they, amid the perils of the field and diseases of the camp, had gone to their rest.

On the third of May, one of the loveliest days of Spring, Hazen's Brigade, of the Third Division, Fourth Army Corps, was encamped near Cleveland, on the railroad leading from

Chattanooga to Knoxville. Early in the day orders were received for a forward move; camps were broken up; all surplus baggage sent to the rear; the troops put in light marching order, one wagon only being allowed to each regiment, which was to transport officers' baggage and ten days' forage for the team. Thus prepared, at twelve o'clock, M., the *assembly* was sounded, which was soon succeeded by the *forward*, at which time the First Brigade moved on, full of glee and cheerfulness, as if on the way to some high festival, instead of the field of danger and of death. In a few moments the Second Brigade, with its distinguished and gallant leader, Hazen, at its head, moved on with that elasticity and precision of step so characteristic of that command, with the watchword, "On to Atlanta!" upon every lip. O, it was a grand sight to behold an army of veterans, whose courage had been proved on many a well-fought field, under the eye of brave and vigilant leaders, with banners frayed and torn in many a deadly struggle, under the cheering notes of the sounding bugle and the inspiration of past success, marching on to dangers greater and fields more glorious than those already won. The day was warm and the march long, and when night overtook us we camped in an open field, wrapped up in our blankets, our only tent the arch of blue, with its glorious stars above.

On the morning of the fourth the boys sprang up at dawn, took their coffee, and were soon ready for the day's march. At six, A. M., the signal to advance rang from the bugles, and the whole command moved forward, but with more caution than on the previous day; our advance-guard had come up with the enemy's pickets, and slight skirmishing continued nearly the whole day. We camped that night near the Catoosa Springs, on the dirt road leading to Tunnel Hill, advanced our pickets, and established our lines within a short distance of the outposts of the enemy.

We remained in camp till the morning of the seventh, during which time some picket firing was kept up, with but little damage to either side. At five o'clock, on the morning of the seventh, our baggage having been further reduced and the surplus sent back to Ringgold, our line moved forward, the Sixth Kentucky in the rear, having been on picket the night before. Our advance-guard soon came in contact with the enemy's skirmishers, who were driven back as far as Tunnel Hill, when, being reënforced, they formed in line of battle and awaited our approach. We did not permit them to wait long; and as our advance moved upon them they opened a heavy fire with artillery and musketry; but finding that they were being flanked on the right by a part of the First Division of the Fourth Army Corps—the Ninth Indiana, I think—they retired in great confusion from their line of works on the top of the hill.

We gained the hill about one o'clock, P. M.;

and during the evening a brisk cannonading was kept up along our lines against some of the enemy, who could be seen across the valley at the base of Rocky Face Mountain, and in the road leading to Buzzard Roost. Our pickets were stationed at the foot of Tunnel Hill, while the Fourth Army Corps camped on its summit—and the rest was all the sweeter for the toils and dangers of the day.

On the next morning all was calm and beautiful, and many of us desired that this quiet, which so well became the Sabbath, would continue through the day; but war is stern work; we had only to look before us in order to see the enemy and their intrenchments upon the summit of Rocky Face. About nine, A. M., our line was formed for a forward movement, which commenced half an hour later — the Sixth Kentucky in the front line. In a few moments the Second Brigade had descended Tunnel Hill, and were rapidly crossing the valley toward Rocky Face. Our advance was resisted, and soon the quiet of the Sabbath was broken by the sounds of battle. We steadily drove the foe across the valley, and camped for the night at the foot of Rocky Face, the enemy occupying the hights above in rifle range of our camp. The evening passed with but little firing, and when night came our boys gathered around the camp-fires as cheerful as if our march were but a pleasure excursion, till the tattoo reminded them of rest needed after the toils of the day, and necessary to prepare them for the conflict of the morrow. Pickets were posted on the mountain-side to watch the movements of the enemy while the army slept; but as soon as day began to dawn the sleepers were aroused by quick, sharp reports from the rifles of the rebel sharp-shooters; their fire called forth corresponding activity on the part of our men, who fired on them with great effect. At eight o'clock, A. M., the Sixth Kentucky advanced as skirmishers; and passing up the mountain-side drove the enemy into the first line of their works upon its summit; which line it would have been madness to attempt to storm, as it was a strong position by nature, and so well fortified in addition that a single line would be amply sufficient to keep an army in check. Our brigade, however, held its advanced position till late in the evening, when it retired slowly and in good order to the foot of the mountain, where we encamped for the night. We lost several men during the day, and next morning were so annoyed by sharpshooters that we were compelled to move our camp to a more secure place across the valley, near the base of Tunnel Hill. Here we remained till the afternoon of the eleventh, during which time constant cannonading and active skirmishing was going on, and matters now began to assume an exciting appearance; a heavy rain fell that day, which made the movement of troops very disagreeable.

In the mean time Sherman, with his flanking columns, was hard at work; and on the night of the twelfth the enemy were compelled to evacuate Rocky Face and Dalton, and pursuit of the retreating foe began the next morning. We marched six miles south of Dalton, and went into camp for the night. Early next morning our line of battle was formed, and the enemy were reported to be awaiting us about three miles from where we stood. Our column moved forward at nine, A. M., and at eleven our advance-guard came up with the rebel skirmishers, who fell back slowly till half-past one, when a general engagement ensued, which lasted till night, and resulted in driving the enemy into his main line of works in front of Resaca. As usual, the Sixth Kentucky held the front rank in the line of battle. During the day our brigade captured a number of prisoners, among them a rebel colonel, and the night was spent in throwing up breast-works, within close rifle range of the enemy's intrenchments. On the morning of the 15th skirmishing commenced, and continued during the day;

at times there was considerable artillery firing, with but little effect, however, on either side. In the afternoon a charge was made on the rebel works by the Second Brigade, which was repelled, with heavy loss on our part. This charge was considered a blunder; it was led by the Colonel of the Fifth Kentucky—a brave man and a good officer. Both men and officers acted nobly in the affair; yet it was a bloody and fruitless attempt to break the rebel lines without assailing their flanks, and should never have been made by a single brigade. It was understood that Gen. Hazen did not favor the movement. Who was in fault may never be known; yet nearly all felt "that some one had blundered;" but wherever the fault may be, it was not with the Second Brigade. That night was one of great and unusual excitement; the enemy evidently was in motion, and thought to be meditating mischief. At one time the impression was that he was advancing upon our camp, and our men stood to their arms—and, to tell the truth, some were fearful; they could fight in daylight, but were somewhat nervous with regard to a night attack. Morning came, and the commotion of the previous night proved to be caused by the enemy abandoning his strong position, and seeking, if not a stronger, at least a safer one further south. We learned then, but, alas! too late, that all the advantages which we gained might have been secured without the loss of the brave men of the Second Brigade; for if compelled to abandon his position after repulsing our attack, he would most certainly have done so had no assault been made. We pursued as soon as we learned of the enemy's flight; but were unable to come up with him, and went into camp six miles south of Resaca.

The town of Resaca is situated on the south side of the Oostanaula River, is surrounded by strong natural defenses, and had been rendered almost impregnable, perhaps entirely so to any army but ours, by admirably-constructed fortifications; but Sherman is such a great fellow for the flanks, or, as the Georgians say, "for coming at them endways," that the army of Johnston was compelled to retire from position to position, till it was only necessary for us to advance in order to insure his retreat. He may be a good general, and unquestionably held some strong positions; but it is now quite evident that a better general was in his rear.

CHAPTER X.

ON TO ATLANTA!

Confidence in our leader—Tunnel Hill and Rocky Face Mountain—Pursuit of the enemy—Johnston's strategy—In command of my regiment—Battle near Dallas—Night on the battle-field—Loss of an officer—Reflections.

WITH some slight reverses our march up to this time was that of a victorious army, and the temporary checks we had met with only served to make us more vigilant for the future. We had the utmost confidence in our leader, which was justified by almost daily successes; while that of the rebels in their chief was daily becoming weaker, in consequence of his failing to make good his promises by a successful stand. And, indeed, when we gained the works which he time after time abandoned, we could not but wonder at the policy which led to the abandonment of works and positions which we felt we could have held against any army that could have been brought against us. In our southward march we were able to understand how it was that the first Napoleon was able to lead an army across the hitherto impassable Alps—it was by infusing into every soldier his own inflexible purpose; the same power is possessed in a high degree by Gen. Sherman; his soldiers think themselves able to execute whatever he commands.

We began our march with the cry, "On to Atlanta! Tunnel Hill and Rocky Face Mountain, deemed impregnable, are already ours! Resaca has fallen into our hands; and there are no difficulties to be surmounted greater than those we have already overcome. Cheer up, cheer up, boys! Atlanta shall soon be ours!"

With such feelings as those just expressed, on the morning of the 17th our army moved on in its conquering march, the men all in fine spirits, and confident of victory whenever the enemy would hazard a general engagement. We passed through Calhoun at eleven, A. M.—skirmishing began about three in the afternoon. We drove the enemy steadily as far as Adairsville, where they had a strong line of works. We began to throw up intrenchments to protect us during the night; the rebels began to shell us furiously while thus engaged; but failing to get the proper range, they did us no harm—our boys laughing gleefully and working zealously as the missiles went shrieking over their heads. We expected hot work in the morning; but when we awoke all was quiet, and we soon made the discovery that the enemy had departed during the night. Our lines were advanced; we entered Adairsville without opposition, and halted there for a few hours—moved forward again five or six miles, and went into camp for the night.

At seven o'clock the next morning we resumed our march, and reached Kingston at ten,

A. M., where we rested an hour or two—the enemy still retreating, hotly pursued, however, by our advance, which had constant skirmishing with their rear-guard.

About one o'clock the enemy made a stand, and our artillery opened upon their line of battle, which was drawn up, apparently in force, in an open field. Our own lines being completed, we advanced upon them and took some prisoners, and drove them till night brought an end to our operations, having during the day driven them past Cassville, and compelled them to take refuge within a strong line of works, where it was reported that they intended to make a final stand. This intelligence was received with great satisfaction by our boys, who began to think that the enemy's strategy was to tire them to death by running after them, and many of them preferred fighting to marching. The Sixth Kentucky was thrown forward into the advance line, where they erected temporary works and spent the night on picket, expecting a battle with the coming light. Day came, but no battle; for, somewhat to our astonishment, after the reports we had heard, Mr. Johnston, as our boys termed the rebel chief, had again executed a night movement, for which he had already become famous—and will you believe it, reader, many were greatly disappointed because there was to be no fighting that day? We remained here two days to rest and replenish our haversacks, as rations had been brought up for a further advance. Our boys enjoyed the rest greatly—especially as they had begun to regard the campaign as a race rather than a conflict, and many were the jests at the expense of our fleet-footed foe, and a general, whose drummer-boys could not say, like the Scotch bagpiper, when asked to play a retreat, "that he had never learned to play *that*."

Up to this time my company had been acting as Provost Guard at head-quarters, in accordance with the expressed wish of Gen.

Hazen; but in consequence of some changes in the regiment, I was sent back to it, with my company, and placed in command; and as this was by order of my brigade commander, Gen. Hazen, under whose eye I had been so long, I could not but esteem it as a great honor; and if I had any ambition to gain the praise of the good and the brave, it most certainly was gratified by an official paper, from which the following is an extract: "Capt. Johnston has always performed duty efficiently; has been in all the battles of the army till captured at Chickamauga; he was shot through and left for dead at Shiloh. He was, with one exception, the most active officer in preparing for, and effecting the escape of a large number of officers recently from Libby Prison." These, and other words still more complimentary, were signed, "W. B. Hazen, Brig.-Gen.;" and it would be affectation in me to say that I was not gratified by the approval of this noble gentleman and good soldier.

Previous to the commencement of the campaign Gen. Hazen had consolidated his brigade into four battalions, each composed of two regiments—each of which, when on the march and in battle, was commanded by the senior officer of the two regiments. The Twenty-Third Kentucky and the Sixth Kentucky were together, and commanded by Lieut.-Col. Foy. Being now in command of the regiment, I shall not attempt the task of giving a full history of the operations of the army during the remainder of the campaign; but content myself with those matters which came under my own eye, in which my own command was concerned.

In obedience to orders, on the 23d of May we broke up our camp before Cassville, and resumed our march southward. The day was very warm, the marching heavy, and we were glad to go into camp, about nine o'clock at night, in a most beautiful country, about five miles south of the Etowah River. Next morning we moved forward and reached the Allatoona Mountains at midday. We rested long enough to make our coffee, then ascended the mountains and camped on the top. Heavy rains fell during the night; the Sixth Kentucky went on picket, and was not relieved till eleven o'clock the next day, at which time the *assembly* was sounded, and the column, on account of the bad roads, moved slowly forward till about six o'clock in the evening, when the sound of cannon was heard, denoting that there was fighting ahead. Our march during the day, though slow, was a pleasant one; the rain of the previous night had cooled the air, the scenery was varied and romantic, and little met our eyes that was suggestive of the terrible ravages of war. But our thoughts were soon diverted from the quiet beauty of the woods and the majestic grandeur of the mountains, by the dread sounds of distant battle. The sounds came from Hooker's Corps, which was in the advance of the flanking movement; and from the cool and tried valor of its veterans, we were prepared to hear of a desperate struggle and fearful carnage. It was even so; this army corps, on its way to Dallas, was met by the enemy in force, and a heavy battle ensued. Hooker suffered greatly; but the steady valor of his men enabled him to hold the field. Our column had orders to push forward; and, through rain and mud, on we pressed till near midnight, meeting on our march sad evidences of the fight—the ambulance and wagon trains, filled with wounded, on their way to the rear, from which, ever and anon, came cries of pain and agony that could not be repressed. We were wet and weary when we received orders to halt, and we lay down in our wet clothing and slept the remainder of the night upon the battle-field, amid the dead and the dying who had fallen in the evening's conflict; yet the thought, I doubt not, passed through many a mind ere slumber came—may I not to-morrow night be like many of those around me who sleep that sleep which knows no waking? Soldiers are generally gay and thoughtless, even in the midst of danger; but they have also their serious moments, and the lightest heart feels sad in the solemn night on the battle-field thickly bestrewn with the dead.

At four in the morning we rose, expecting a hard day's work; for picket firing was kept up all night, and increased after daylight. At seven o'clock we were in line of battle—the Sixth Kentucky in front. Companies D and F were thrown forward as skirmishers, while the rest of the regiment was building breast-works, and while thus engaged suffered considerably from the enemy's sharp-shooters. Selecting a number of the best shots in my command, I assigned them the task of silencing them, which was soon accomplished. At one o'clock the whole regiment advanced, driving the enemy's skirmishers within their works, and established our own lines in close rifle range of them, and during the night, by dint of hard labor, we intrenched ourselves securely. During the evening, while on the skirmish line, and occupying the extreme left, we were threatened by the rebel cavalry, against which I sent a few men under the charge of a lieutenant, and dispatched a messenger to Gen. Hazen, notifying him of my condition. On his way back the messenger was wounded by a rebel sharp-shooter, and was taken to the rear; but the message he was bearing was brought to me—it was, that Gen. Schofield's command would soon join me on the left, and that I must hold my advanced position till he made his appearance, which I did till near sundown, when the Twenty-Third Corps came up, and my weary flankers were relieved.

Early on the morning of the 27th the regiment was relieved from duty on the front line, and moved back a short distance to rest, which was greatly needed; and while preparing some coffee, a man belonging to the battery was wounded. Lieut. William Furr, myself, and two others, were placing the wounded man in a litter, and while thus engaged Lieut. Furr received a wound which in a few days proved fatal. He was a brave man and good officer, and his loss was much regretted. Such incidents are the frequent and sad episodes in a soldier's life, and make an impression deep and lasting — the very dangers and toils through which they pass bind them together with a power only understood by those who have been partakers of this fellowship of suffering. The soldier often seems gay and light-hearted in immediate prospect of a battle; and I have seen a regiment express as much joy when the loud guns announced the approach of a fierce conflict, as school-boys would at an unexpected vacation; and yet those same men will at other times be as tender and tearful as women. When they look down the lines, thinned in many a battle; or, by the nightly camp-fire, talk of comrades gone; or wrap in his overcoat or blanket the remains of one who has borne with them the fatigues of the march or the perils of the fight, and make his grave in a land of strangers, the bosom heaves, the tears fall, and every look and tone proclaims that under the soldier's garb a true human heart is beating still.

CHAPTER XI.

MARCHING AND FIGHTING.

Reminder to the reader—Sherman, Howard, and Thomas in council—The attack and repulse—The Sixth Kentucky in front again—In the trenches—Guarding train—Forward march.

I MUST remind the reader that I did not set out with the intention of giving a history of the grand campaign in which I took a humble part—a task of such magnitude and responsibility must be reserved for the future historian of one of the greatest and most complicated struggles that the world has witnessed. Indeed, the thoughtful reader, a thousand miles from the scene of strife, may have a better conception of a great battle than many of those engaged in it. The former, by the aid of maps, and the accounts given by various writers who beheld the different parts of the great struggle, may get a good general idea of it as a whole; while he who takes part in it, of necessity, sees only that portion of the battle in which he is engaged—and that generally is but a small part. Moreover, he is prone to judge of the result by the success, or suffering, of the regiment or brigade with which he is connected; while all are aware that a portion of an army may meet with great disaster, and yet the general result may be most glorious; but glorious it certainly does not seem to that portion of the army which has suffered most severely, although its suffering may have been the salvation of the rest. For instance, the celebrated charge made by Marshal Macdonald against the Austrian center at Wagram; although it turned the day in favor of the French army, yet it was most disastrous to the charging column, which is said to have lost in the proportion of ten out of every eleven men who composed it, not having as many hundreds in its ranks when the task was achieved as it had thousands when the word to charge was given. Thus, in some of the battles of this campaign, a brigade, and even a division, at times suffers terribly, and yet the battle was not lost, and the enterprise, as a whole, was a splendid success.

This view of affairs is absolutely necessary with regard to some matters in the present chapter which it is necessary to mention, as I am not attempting a general view of the campaign, but the part played in it by the brigade to which I was attached, and more particularly by my own regiment; and while not writing a history, I am preparing materials to be used by others in framing a full and perfect account of this truly-wonderful march. I write chiefly from what came under my own notice—those who were in other scenes than those in which I took part will do the same; and the truth must be gathered, not from any one account, taken separately, but from all the accounts in the aggregate. If, then, I speak of a success, do not think it was one achieved by the whole army; if I mention a disaster, let no one think that I regard the whole army as involved in it; for seldom has an expedition of like proportions met fewer reverses, or more glorious success.

About seven o'clock, on the morning of the 27th of May, a group of officers were assembled in front of the Sixth Kentucky, engaged in deep and earnest conversation. Although we could not hear their words, their looks and manners indicated that matters of grave import were occupying their attention. One of the group, though his garb indicated no great rank, had the look of one born to command; his face lighted up with unmistakable tokens of genius as he spoke, and his words seemed most convincing. Another had a calm, quiet face, with a look that showed great goodness of heart; yet he was evidently a good soldier, as his empty sleeve showed that he had lost an arm in defense of his country's flag. A third was a plain, unpretending-looking personage; yet the lines of determination upon his rugged face showed there was, under that quiet exterior, an invincible will. They were in the order I have described them—Sherman, one of the greatest military geniuses of the age; Howard, the man without fear and without reproach; and Thomas, who stood up so stoutly at Chickamauga, and many other well-fought fields. These, with other general officers, were planning the operations of the day; and having decided upon the course to be pursued, the interview ended, and each one returned to his respective command.

I was informed by a member of Gen. Howard's staff that we might look for hot work, as a general advance would soon be made upon the rebel works. Our brigade was immediately moved about a mile to the left, and formed in two lines of battle—the Sixth Kentucky forming the extreme left of the rear line. At ten o'clock the advance was sounded. With the belief that we should engage the enemy at once, my orders were to support the regiment before me in the front line of battle. Our lines advanced slowly, and we had not gone far before skirmishing began. But instead of a general engagement, as was expected, it seemed more like a brigade drill; for, as we passed over the broken country which was the scene of operations, every movement was preceded and indicated by Willich's brigade bugles, which must have intimated to the enemy what we were about. It was soon whispered that we were searching for the enemy's right flank. About three o'clock we reached what was thought to be the desired point; here the column halted till Johnson's Division moved up and formed in our rear, making four lines of battle. When we first came up we found a picket-post of the enemy established at that point, which was fired upon by our advance and driven back, and no enemy was now in view. The "attention" was sounded, all were ready in line of battle, and in a moment more the order "double-quick" rang out. All moved forward; the front line changed direction to the right, while the second line moved forward, which soon brought it into the front line of battle—the Sixth Kentucky being on the extreme left, and in the second line of battle, with orders to support the front line—which orders had not been countermanded. I had not been informed that the front line had been changed; nor could I see, on account of the dense thickets through which we were moving, that the change had been made; and the first thing that apprised me of the change was passing over the skirmish line amid a perfect storm of rebel bullets, and finding myself and command in the front line of battle. On we pressed till we came to an open field, on the opposite side of which the rebels were strongly posted. The right of our brigade was to cross this field, while part of the Twenty-Third Kentucky, and the right wing of the Sixth Kentucky was formed diagonally across it, and the left wing of the Sixth was formed front to rear to meet a flanking column of the enemy that was moving to our rear. This movement on the part of the enemy would have been successful had I not at that moment formed my left wing so as to return the flanking fire he was already pouring into us. The battle now raged furiously along our line, and, under a murderous fire, the rebels were pressed back to their works, our troops following, in some instances, to within fifteen or twenty paces of the intrenchments; but exposed as they were in an open field to the deadly volleys of a protected foe, and a fierce fire upon the flanks—shattered, torn, and bleeding, yet in spirit unconquered, they fell back to the shelter of the woods. Taking a position there, the battle was renewed, and an attempt was made on the part of the enemy to dislodge them, but the failure was most signal. Some idea of the dreadful carnage may be formed from the fact, that in a space of time nearly as brief as it has taken to pen these few lines, our division lost nearly fifteen hundred men. Our division went into the fight alone, and was not supported by the division formed in its rear. After reaching the point of attack the fight was put off two hours; and when it began the enemy had time to mass three divisions against one of ours. I am of the opinion that had the attack been made at once the day would have been ours.

Great as was our loss, it proved but a barren victory to the enemy. We were repulsed, it is true, and many of our brave men sealed their devotion to their country with their blood. The enemy also lost heavily, and their success was due to their greatly-superior numbers; and whatever advantage they gained that day, it was not sufficient to check the advance of our army; for they were soon again on the retreat, and our army on the march to victory.

But I must return to my own command. After our repulse I was at the extreme left with a few men who were still firing, when Lieut. Clark, Acting Adjutant, came up and told me that the brigade had been relieved, and was now assembling at the place where the charge began. I knew nothing of its withdrawal, and replied that he must certainly be mistaken. He said there was no mistake about it, that all the brigade colors were at the place he had mentioned—that we were relieved beyond a doubt. Still uncertain, I asked, "Where are the troops to relieve us? I don't see them; but if relieved I will go down to the left, where I have some men placed; and after relieving them will go back." Lieut. Clark, who is a brave young officer, went with me, and told them to go back, as our brigade had gone to the rear; and on our way we passed the relief, which was lying down, and had not come to our relief at all—a mere handful of us had remained on the field, and the wonder is that we were not captured to a man.

When we reached the brigade we found it formed and ready to march to the rear, with Gen. Hazen at its head; but O, how changed! In a few hours it was so cut down as to be not larger than a regiment. We were moved down to Pumpkin Vine Creek; but were not suffered to remain there long, being ordered to the front, and to the right of where the battle had taken place; and though we had been engaged in skirmish duty nearly two days before the battle, we took our place in the front, and began building works within rifle range of the enemy's lines.

At this point we remained till the 6th of June, during which time nothing took place of interest, save the usual picket duty, of which our regiment did its full share. Our position, however, was very unpleasant on account of the heavy rains which fell, and being compelled to lay close in our trenches to shelter ourselves from the rebel sharp-shooters, who were always on the alert.

On the night of the 5th of June the rebels evacuated their works in front of us, Gen. Sherman having executed another flank movement which rendered it necessary for them to retreat. By sunrise the next morning we advanced again over roads rendered very bad by the recent rains, and on the next day were detailed, with the Twenty-Third Kentucky, to Carterville, to guard a train down to the army. We were absent till the morning of the 10th, having marched all the previous night in order to get the supplies through as soon as possible. When we reached camp we found the army ready to march; but it was delayed till two, P. M. We then moved forward about three miles, and halted for the night.

CHAPTER XII.

SHERMAN STILL FLANKING.

Pine Mountain, and death of Gen. Polk—Georgia scenery—Before Kenesaw—The unreturning brave—Marietta ours—Across the Chattahoochee.

On the morning of the eleventh all was quiet. At an early hour we advanced one mile, and formed in line of battle in front of the enemy; and no demonstration having been made against us, we were withdrawn at night, and went into camp till the 14th, during which time nothing of interest took place, save the arrival of the cars at Big Shanty with rations; and it made all feel better to know that we were not expected to march and fight upon empty stomachs.

At noon on the 14th our division struck camp and marched to the left three miles, formed our line of battle, and remained there till the next day. Some skirmishing took place in front of Pine Mountain, on which the rebel Gen. Polk was killed on the evening of the 14th. He was one of the Bishops of the Episcopal Church before the war, and possessed great influence in the South. In the army he had attained the rank of Lieutenant-General, and was esteemed an able officer. In company with some other commanders he had taken a position on the mountain to observe our movements, when one of our batteries opened upon them; they withdrew for a time, but curiosity drew them back; and while engaged in conversation with his companions, a shell struck him on the left arm, and passed through his chest; of course he was killed instantly. These particulars were obtained from a rebel officer who fell into our hands a few days after.

On the 17th I ascended the mountain, the enemy having evacuated it, and visited the spot where he fell. While there I had a fine view of Lost and Kenesaw Mountains; and when I looked at their steep sides from which their batteries were belching shot and shell, it really seemed madness to think of attempting to make them our own. Others might have looked at them with the eye of a tourist; but I looked at them with reference to the difficulties which they presented to our advance. Viewed as mere scenery, they present a grand and imposing spectacle; but I thought of Tunnel Hill and Rocky Face, and the struggle they had cost us, and then thought of the lives that must be sacrificed before those embattled hights which frowned before me could be ours. Mountains are beautiful, sublime, and all that; to ascend them with pleasant company and in delightful weather, and gaze from the summit at the lovely landscape below, is full of delight; but we soldiers think of the sheets of flame and the storm of bullets through which we must press our way before those summits, standing out so boldly in the sunlight, can be gained.

On the 17th we advanced over two lines of rebel works which were evacuated the previous night; but soon were compelled to form in line of battle, having come up with the enemy's pickets in front of their strong fortifications— the Sixth Kentucky in the front line as usual. We advanced slowly till night, driving the skirmishers into their works, and advancing our own lines within close range of the enemy's rifle pits, and spent most of the night in throwing up works to protect ourselves, our position being quite an exposed one in an open field. Next morning the rain began to fall, and continued without intermission during the day; this, however, did not prevent constant skirmishing and cannonading. About two o'clock the enemy opened a battery which enfiladed our line of works, rendering our position rather a warm one, notwithstanding the drenching rain to which we were exposed. We remained here till sundown, and were relieved only to take a position still further to the front, where we had to build another line of works during the night, in an open field, within close range of the rebel sharp-shooters. I do not remember ever having known as much rain to fall in a single day as on the preceding one; we had been two days in the front line without being relieved, and were obliged to cut green corn and weeds to keep us out of the mud and water of the trenches, when we lay down for a few moments' rest. Early next morning our skirmishers were thrown forward, who soon returned and reported that the enemy had left during the night; a number of deserters came into our lines during the day, and we also captured a number of prisoners.

The enemy were driven that day to their works at the foot of Kenesaw Mountain, and troops were in motion, and cannonading kept up all night. In the morning the Sixth Kentucky was relieved from picket, and formed in the front line, working at the intrenchments till two o'clock, P. M., having been on picket duty the twenty-four hours previous; and then, wearied as we were with labor on the breastworks, were ordered into the front line of battle. All this, however, was done cheerfully, and the rebels were driven into their rifle pits, and our line of battle established within six hundred yards of their works. Here we fortified ourselves and remained till the second of July, when Kenesaw Mountain was evacuated.

During all that time we had fighting, more or less, every day; our picket lines were within seventy-five yards of the enemy's, and it was dangerous for a man on either side to show his head above the works. Our regiment was on picket every other day, as was every regiment in our brigade—our lines being weakened to enable Gen. Sherman to feel the enemy's flanks.

On the 23d of June Companies H and K were on picket, when it was ordered to make a demonstration in our front; the line was to advance at five, P. M., supported by the Ninety-Third Ohio Volunteer Infantry. In obedience to orders the advance was made. Capt. Owen was in command of the picket; but before they moved I was ordered to send another officer to his assistance, and sent Capt. Nierhoff. Our boys had scarcely got from behind their works when the enemy opened a galling fire upon them; they advanced the line, however, to the rifle pits, but with the loss of fifteen men out of the thirty-five that were engaged—among the killed was Capt. Nierhoff. Company H had four killed and eight wounded; Company K had two wounded; the Ninety-Third Ohio lost forty-three in killed and wounded. We held the position which we had gained at such a sacrifice till dark, when our lines were withdrawn to their original position. The bravery of the men was put to a severe test by this movement; but it was, beyond doubt, ill-advised, as every man knew that we were in full range of the rebels' main line of works.

Several fierce contests took place while we were in front of Kenesaw Mountain—one of the bloodiest of which took place on our left, the sad and sickening traces of which remained till the enemy retreated. On the night that the enemy evacuated their stronghold, our brigade was ordered to relieve some troops on our left, and my regiment was placed in the front line, so close to the enemy that each party did picket duty from the main line of their respective works, which were not more than one hundred yards apart. Across this narrow space two charges had been made—one by the rebels, the other by our men, in each case with severe loss to the charging column; and the intervening space was now, several days after the battle, thickly strewn with the swollen, disfigured, and putrefying bodies of the gallant dead upon the very spot where they fell—blue jackets and gray all intermingled, all silent and peaceful in their last sleep, presenting the saddest spectacle I had witnessed amid all the dreadful scenes of the war. The carnage must have been terrible; but the gray uniforms far outnumbered the blue on that sad field of the slain. The reason why they were left unburied is said to have been the refusal of the rebel officer commanding that part of the line to receive a flag of truce—such a wretch deserves neither a soldier's grave nor a soldier's tear.

On the 3d of July the army moved in pursuit of the retreating foe; and after marching ten miles went into camp near the railroad south of Marietta. All was quiet for the first time for two weeks. The evacuation of Kenesaw threw Marietta into our hands, which was occupied immediately as a depot for supplies, and for the use of our sick and wounded. This is said to be one of the most beautiful of Southern cities, the town being well built, and the suburbs adorned with dwellings eminently suggestive of comfort within, and they certainly are outwardly beautiful. The Georgia Military Institute occupies a beautiful and commanding situation south of the town, and the inhabitants are a much superior class of people to any we had as yet met with in our march through the State.

The scenery in the vicinity possesses the great charm of variety—lovely valleys and mountains sublime — Kenesaw, Altoona, and Lost Mountains being all in full view. Before the war this was quite a manufacturing point. Churches and school-houses are more abundant than in most portions of the South through which I have passed, and I am convinced there are also not a few Union men.

On the morning of the 4th of July our brigade moved a mile to the left, the enemy being near at hand. Line of battle was formed, with the Sixth in the front line; fighting all day, the foe before us in force and strongly fortified. We held our position till next morning, when it was ascertained that Sherman had again succeeded in his favorite flank movement, and the enemy was again forced to leave his strongholds and fall back, this time over Chattahoochee River, into the first lines of his strong works for the defense of Atlanta—only eight miles distant. The pursuit then began—my regiment in the advance. During the day we came up with their rear-guard, had some fighting, and captured some prisoners, and reached the river in time to prevent the rebels from destroying the bridge over which they crossed near Vining's Station. After a little fighting, with the river between us, we were ordered to fall back and pitch our camp. We remained there till the 10th, our pickets on the north bank and the rebel pickets on the south. Here we stopped five days; our batteries were located at the best points, and the most furious cannonade that I had yet heard was kept up both day and night. The sharp-shooters, too, were busy; nor did the rebels permit us to do all the shooting with the big guns; but planting their batteries, they fired with great precision—at one time obtaining such a good range on the camp of the Sixth Kentucky as to wound several of my men. At some points on the river some of our boys and the "rebs" would get up an armistice, and gray jackets and blue jackets would meet and mingle in the greatest harmony, and in an hour or two would be pouring a deadly fire into each other's ranks.

Our next move was to the left, and up the river, to effect a crossing. We marched seven miles, and went into camp. The next day we were ordered to cross; but when we reached the river we found the bridge was not completed, which delayed us several hours. We got over at length, marched about a mile and a half, and went into camp. Next morning we changed our position, moving forward, and to the right, upon an elevated point, upon which we soon erected a strong line of works, behind which we lay till the 17th, when the Third Division of the Fourth Army Corps was ordered to move down the south side of the Chattahoochee as far as Vining's Station, to dislodge the enemy, who was then in front of the Fourteenth Corps, and hold the crossing till the pontoons were laid and the army across. This we accomplished without the loss of a man, and succeeded also in capturing some prisoners; and having finished our work, returned the same night to our camp.

CHAPTER XIII.

BEFORE ATLANTA.

Intrenching all night—Gallant exploit of the First and Third Brigades—Atlanta in view—In the trenches before the city—The Sixth Kentucky ordered to Tennessee—Turning over my command—A parting word.

EARLY on the morning of the 18th marching orders were received, and at eight o'clock, A. M., our brigade moved forward over a rough road, our advance constantly engaged with the pickets of the enemy, who retired before them. On reaching the Cross Roads we effected a junction with Hooker's Corps, and formed in line of battle, the rebels being in force in our front. We went to work and threw up intrenchments; but the position assigned to the Sixth Kentucky did not suit the commanding officer, and we were obliged to advance and erect another line of works, which occupied us most of the night. This is a kind of work under which soldiers often become restive; and, indeed, it is far from agreeable, after a hard day's marching and fighting, to find, after some hours of toil in throwing up works, that the line has been improperly located, that a new one must be chosen, and the balance of the night spent in work that might have been avoided by a little care in the selection of the position. When the second line also fails to please, as is sometimes the case, the remarks of the soldiers are not very complimentary to the skill and military sagacity of the officer whose blunder has cost them so much labor and loss of necessary sleep; and the wish is often expressed that Gen. —— had the selection of the position, as his eye never fails to see the proper place at the first glance.

On the morning of the 19th our brigade moved to Peach Tree Creek, in support of the First and Third Brigades, while they attempted to cross the stream. This they did handsomely in the face of a heavy fire, forcing the enemy to abandon a strong line of works—possessing them so hastily as to capture a lieutenant-colonel, several line officers, and nearly an entire regiment in the trenches. This, in high military circles, is regarded as one of the most brilliant achievements of the campaign, and reflects the highest credit on the noble men by whom it was accomplished.

While the First and Third Brigades were engaged in converting the rebel works just gained by their valor into Federal defenses, our brigade, under Gen. Hazen, was employed in constructing two bridges for the artillery and wagons to cross upon. After dark we passed over and relieved the troops in the front line, after a hard and exciting day's work, which was attended, however, with but little loss. On the next day our division was relieved from this portion of the line by Newton's Division, of the

Fourth Army Corps, and moved some ten miles to the left, on the north side of Peach Tree Creek, and, for the first time in a long while, enjoyed the luxury of a quiet night's rest—there being troops in our front, which relieved us of any fears of a night attack.

On the 21st we advanced to Peach Tree Creek, built a bridge and crossed, soon after which we came up with the enemy strongly intrenched. Our column halted, formed line of battle, and began throwing up defenses in front. This, however, was done under a sharp fire, and before our works were completed several men of my now greatly-reduced regiment fell. We occupied this position till the next day, when we found the enemy had decamped, Sherman having rendered such a movement on their part a necessity. Gen. Wood ordered us to advance at once, adding that we must throw out a strong line of skirmishers, move on, and stop for nothing till we had reached Atlanta; and had we been able to carry his order out, we should have been ere nightfall possessors of the Gate City. There was one difficulty in the way, however—the enemy was unwilling that we should do so, and had only left one line of works to occupy another stronger one, behind which they thought themselves more secure from the encroaching Yankees. I was ordered to move the Sixth forward as skirmishers, and did so till we came upon the enemy strongly intrenched, and established our picket line in close rifle range of the enemy. This position I held till our battle line advanced, during which time the rebels gave my line a most terrific shelling; but this was no novelty to the brave boys of the Sixth; they swerved not for a moment, and before the sun went down the line of our brigade was strongly intrenched, our batteries in position, and hurling their deadly volleys upon the lines of the foe, and upon Atlanta itself.

Now, for the first time since the campaign began, the Sixth Kentucky was permitted to rest for a season. Our boys dug pits in the ground to protect themselves from the shells and minie balls which the enemy distributed profusely, waiting anxiously for the fall of the city which had been the object of so much labor and suffering, but which seemed to be in our grasp at last. Here we remained, with but little change in our position, and that an advanced one, for over three weeks; and yet, as the fox-hunters say, we were not in at the death; for, on the 21st of August, I received orders to report the regiment to Gen. Rosseau, at Decherd, Tenn., having been transferred from the Fourth Army Corps to the Twentieth.

During the time we were in front of Atlanta, we were almost constantly under the enemy's fire, both musketry and artillery. Our lines were in an open field, while those of the rebels were in the timber on the opposite side, the pickets from each side being advanced into the open field, and at close range, especially after we had driven them from their first line of forts and occupied them ourselves.

Though enjoying comparative rest when contrasted with our toils on the march, we were by no means idle; we were engaged in picket duty, in building and strengthening our defenses, skirmishing, and making demonstrations against the enemy; and toward the close of our stay, when our works were completed, we drilled twice a day in an open field, within range of rebel sharp-shooters.

In obedience to General Orders of the War Department, I made application for Companies A, B, and C to return to the rear preparatory to being mustered out of service, as the regiment will have served three years on the 1st of October—and that, too, in the front, from Shiloh to the Gate City of the sunny South; but, for want of being mustered at the proper time, they will have to serve till the 23d of December, 1864. I requested that the remaining seven companies should be sent to Eminence, Ky., where they were partly organized, to watch after the notorious rebel Jessee, and his gang. This, however, was not granted; but, as already stated, we were transferred to the Twentieth Army Corps, to report at Decherd, Tenn. On the 23d of August we reached Chattanooga, and I turned over the command to an officer who certainly did not owe his place in the regiment to his faithful discharge of duty; for he knew little, practically, of the dangers through which it had passed, not being with it in the campaign in which it had played so distinguished a part. The regiment was drawn up in line, and I returned thanks to officers and men for the faithful discharge of their duty in the campaign against Atlanta, and referred to the imperishable record they had made. Cheers arose all along the line; scarcely a man in the regiment was silent; and never shall I forget this warm expression of their confidence and regard. To my own company, in particular, I feel deeply indebted; to them I owe the position I occupied through the most remarkable campaign of the war; and with them I shall remain, if life be spared, till we reach home again. The day for our return is not far distant; but O, how few of those who started with me, nearly three years ago, will return! Many parents will weep over sons, and wives over husbands, who will return no more; but they died in a holy cause, and have left a name which those who mourn their loss may cherish with pride. During the campaign against Atlanta alone the regiment lost, in killed and wounded, fifty-eight out of one hundred and forty who were engaged; and when mustered out the ranks will be thin, the numbers few. Not many regiments have seen harder service than ours—none have borne themselves more nobly; and I cherish the thought that my little book may be useful to the historian of the war in Georgia and Tennessee, as the record of the doings of the noble Sixth Kentucky.

I regret my inability to give a full list of the losses sustained by the regiment; a few names, however, which now occur I will mention. Lieut.-Col. Cotton was killed at the battle of Stone River, on the 30th of December, 1862. Adjutant Middleton died in the hospital—an accomplished Christian gentleman, and soldier brave and true. Orderly-Sergeant W. H. Harper was badly wounded at Chickamauga; and among the killed of my company were Sergeant G. W. Lindsey, James Downs, and John H. Hall. On the 24th of December my time, and that of my company, will expire; and I trust, ere that day dawns, that bright-winged, dove-eyed peace, with the olive twig just plucked off, will return. But if this may not be, I shall not feel that I am discharged from further duty. The feeble efforts I have made in my country's cause have been made freely; I regret not the wounds I have received, or the cruel imprisonment I have endured; and if peace, an honorable peace, be not obtained, I am willing to pass through yet greater perils that my country may triumph. That triumph will come at last, I can not doubt; the justice of our cause and the spirit of our soldiers assures me of this. We have met with defeat and disaster on some occasions, it is true; yet our cause has ever been advancing. We have had many cases of individual suffering, and yet those who have suffered most have never despaired. Amid the privation and starvation of Libby Prison I never found any who regretted the part they had taken in this struggle, or who for a moment doubted the glorious result. As Paul and Silas sang praises at midnight in the recesses of the Philippian jail, so did they nobly bear all they suffered, sustained by the firm conviction that the cause in which they had periled all was a just one, and would prevail at last.

And now, reader, we must part; and if I have awakened in your breast a stronger sympathy for the soldier in the field, and the captive in prison, we have not met in vain. Should peace speedily come, you may conclude that I have turned the sword into the plowshare; but if the war must go on, you may safely conclude that I am a soldier for the Union still.

EVERY-NAME INDEX

AKERLY, Capt 118
BEAUREGARD, 25 27 Gen 24
BRAGG, 26 27 33 Gen 36
BUELL, 25 27
BUTLER, Gen 109 113 117 125
CARLSON, R 13
CLARK, Capt 65 95 Lt 164
COTTON, Lt-Col 189
DAVIS, Gen 29
DAVY, Lt 88 96
DOWNS, James 189
FISLAR, 114 Lt 65 66 79 89 96 111 119
FITZSIMMONS, Maj 55 63 88 95 121
FOSTER, Lt 96
FOY, Lt-Col 148
FURR, Lt 153 William 152
GALLAGHER, Capt 55 58 63 82 95 121
GARFIELD, 34
GRANT, 27 Gen 23 24
HALL, John H 189

HAMILTON, Capt 55 56 58 63 86 90 95
HARPER, W H 189
HAZEN, 131 132 Gen 139 146-148 152 165 182 W B 147
HOOKER, 149 150 180
HOWARD, 155 159 Gen 159
JESSEE, 187
JOHNSON, 160
JOHNSTON, 25 27 141 142 146 A S 24 Capt 147 I N 96 J J 130
LEE, Gen 53
LINDSEY, G W 189
LONGSTREET, 34 38 39 41
LUCAS, Capt 65 95
LYTLE, 34
M'ALPINE, George 124
M'CLERNAND, 24
M'DONALD, Maj 65 73 86 95
M'KEE, Lt 73
MACDONALD, Marshal 156
MIDDLETON, Adjutant 189

MILROY, Gen 57
MITCHELL, Lt 96
MONTFORT, Mr 129
MORGAN, John 56
NASH, Annie 131
NEWTON, 182
NIERHOFF, Capt 173
OWEN, Capt 173
PALMER, Lt 119
POLK, Gen 168
PRENTISS, 24
RANDALL, Capt 83
RANDELL, Capt 84 96
ROSE, Col 95
ROSECRANS, 27 37

ROSSEAU, Gen 185
SCHOFIELD, Gen 152
SHERMAN, 24 127 137 141 155 159 176 183 Gen 143 166 172
SIMPSON, Lt 96
STERLING, Lt 96
STREIGHT, Col 57 74
THOMAS, 34 155 159 Gen 33
TURNER, Maj 73
WALLACE, Gen 24
WILLICH, 160
WISTAR, Gen 124
WOOD, Gen 183

www.ingramcontent.com/pod-product-compliance
Lightning Source LLC
Chambersburg PA
CBHW071422160426
43195CB00013B/1774